IF NOT, WINTER

IF NOT, WINTER

FRAGMENTS OF SAPPHO

T R A N S L A T E D

B Y

ANNE CARSON

VINTAGE BOOKS

A DIVISION OF RANDOM HOUSE, INC.

NEW YORK

Grateful acknowledgment is made to Em. Querido's Uitgeverij B.V. for permission to
reprint excerpts from *Sappho et Alcaeus* by Eva-Maria Voigt. Reprinted by permission
of Em. Querido's Uitgeverij B.V., Amsterdam.

The Library of Congress has cataloged the Knopf edition as follows:

Sappho.

If not, winter : fragments of Sappho / translated by Anne Carson.—1st ed.

p.   cm.

Poetry in English and Greek.

ISBN 0-375-41067-8 (alk. paper)

1. Sappho—Translations into English.   2. Lesbos Island (Greece)—Poetry.

3. Women—Greece—Poetry. I. Carson, Anne, 1950– II. Title.

PA4408.E5 C37 2002

884'.01—dc21

2001050247

Vintage ISBN: 0-375-72451-6

Book design by Carol Devine Carson and Gabriele Wilson

www.vintagebooks.com

Printed in the United States of America

10   9   8   7   6   5   4   3   2

CONTENTS

WITH SPECIAL THANKS TO

DOROTA DUTSCH

INTRODUCTION

ON SAPPHO

Sappho was a musician. Her poetry is *lyric,* that is, composed to be sung to the lyre. She addresses her lyre in one of her poems (fr. 118) and frequently mentions music, songs and singing. Ancient vase painters depict her with her instrument. Later writers ascribe to her three musical inventions: that of the *plectron,* an instrument for picking the lyre *(Suda);* that of the *pektis,* a particular kind of lyre (Athenaios *Deipnosophistai* 14.635b); and the mixolydian mode, an emotional mode also used by tragic poets, who learned it from Sappho (Aristoxenos cited by Plutarch *On Music* 16.113c). All Sappho's music is lost.

Sappho was also a poet. There is a fifth-century *hydria* in the National Museum of Athens that depicts Sappho, identified by name, reading from a papyrus. This is an ideal image; whether or not she herself was literate is unknown. But it seems likely that the words to her songs were written down during or soon after her lifetime and existed on papyrus rolls by the end of the fifth century B.C. On a papyrus roll the text is written in columns, without word division, punctuation or lineation. To read such a text is hard even when it comes to us in its entirety and most papyri don't. Of the nine books of lyrics that Sappho is said to have composed, one poem has survived complete. All the rest are fragments.

Sappho lived in the city of Mytilene on the island of Lesbos from about 630 B.C. It is not known when she died. Her exile to Sicily sometime between 604 and 595 B.C. is mentioned in an ancient inscription (the Parian Marble) but no reason for it is given. Biographical sources mention a mother, a father, a daughter, a husband and three brothers of Sappho. She appears to have devoted her life to composing songs; scholars in Alexandria collected them in nine books, of which the first book alone had 1320 lines. Most of this is lost. Her face was engraved on the coinage of Mytilene (see G. M. A. Richter, *Portraits of the Greeks,* I.70–72) and Hellenistic poets called her "the tenth Muse" or "the mortal Muse" (see *Palatine Anthology* 9.506 and 7.14). The general tenor of ancient opinion on her work is summarized by a remark of Strabo:

Sappho [is] an amazing thing. For we know
in all of recorded history not one woman
who can even come close to rivaling her
in the grace of her poetry.

(13.2.3)

Controversies about her personal ethics and way of life have taken up a lot of
people's time throughout the history of Sapphic scholarship. It seems that she
knew and loved women as deeply as she did music. Can we leave the matter there?
As Gertrude Stein says:

She ought to be a very happy woman. Now we are able to recognize a photo-
graph. We are able to get what we want.

—"Marry Nettie," *Gertrude Stein Writings 1903–1932*
(New York, 1999), 461

ON THE TEXT

Breaks are always, and fatally, reinscribed in an old cloth that must continually, inter-
minably be undone.

—J. Derrida, *Positions* (Chicago, 1981), 24

In general the text of this translation is based on *Sappho et Alcaeus: Fragmenta,*
edited by Eva-Maria Voigt (Amsterdam, 1971). I include all the fragments printed
by Voigt of which at least one word is legible; on occasion I have assumed variants
or conjectures from her apparatus into my translation and these are discussed
below (see Notes). In translating I tried to put down all that can be read of each
poem in the plainest language I could find, using where possible the same order of
words and thoughts as Sappho did. I like to think that, the more I stand out of the
way, the more Sappho shows through. This is an amiable fantasy (transparency of
self) within which most translators labor. If light appears

not ruining the eyes (as Sappho says)
but strengthening, nourishing and watering

—Aelius Aristides *Orations* 18.4

we undo a bit of the cloth.

ON MARKS AND LACKS

Sappho's fragments are of two kinds: those preserved on papyrus and those derived from citation in ancient authors. When translating texts read from papyri, I have used a single square bracket to give an impression of missing matter, so that] or [indicates destroyed papyrus or the presence of letters not quite legible somewhere in the line. It is not the case that every gap or illegibility is specifically indicated: this would render the page a blizzard of marks and inhibit reading. Brackets are an aesthetic gesture toward the papyrological event rather than an accurate record of it. I have not used brackets in translating passages, phrases or words whose existence depends on citation by ancient authors, since these are intentionally incomplete. I emphasize the distinction between brackets and no brackets because it will affect your reading experience, if you allow it. Brackets are exciting. Even though you are approaching Sappho in translation, that is no reason you should miss the drama of trying to read a papyrus torn in half or riddled with holes or smaller than a postage stamp—brackets imply a free space of imaginal adventure.

A duller load of silence surrounds the bits of Sappho cited by ancient scholiasts, grammarians, metricians, etc., who want a dab of poetry to decorate some proposition of their own and so adduce *exempla* without context. For instance, the second-century-A.D. grammarian Apollonios Dyskolos, who composed a treatise *On Conjunctions* in which he wished to make a point about the spelling of the interrogative particle in different dialects of ancient Greek, cites from Sappho this verse:

> Do I still long for my virginity?
> —Apollonios Dyskolos *On Conjunctions* 490 = Sappho fr. 107 Voigt

Whose virginity? It would be nice to know whether this question comes from a wedding song (and so likely an impersonation of the voice of the bride) or not (and so possibly a personal remark of Sappho's). Apollonios Dyskolos is not interested in such matters. Or consider the third-century-B.C. philosopher Chrysippos whose treatise *On Negatives* includes this negation from Sappho:

> Not one girl I think who looks on the light of the sun will ever have wisdom like this.
> —Chrysippos *On Negatives* 13 = Sappho fr. 56 Voigt

Wisdom like what? And who is this girl? And why is Sappho praising her? Chrysippos is not concerned with anything except Sappho's sequence of negative adverbs. There is also the second-century-A.D. lexicographer Pollux whose lexicon includes the following entry:

> A word *beudos* found in Sappho is the same as the word *kimberikon* which means a short transparent dress.
>
> —Pollux 7.49 = Sappho fr. 177 Voigt

Who would not like to know more about this garment? But the curiosity of Pollux is strictly lexical. In translating such stranded verse I have sometimes manipulated its spacing on the page, to restore a hint of musicality or suggest syntactic motion. For example the sentence cited by Chrysippos becomes:

> not one girl I think
> who looks on the light of the sun
> will ever
> have wisdom
> like this

This is a license undertaken in deference to a principle that Walter Benjamin calls "the intention toward language" of the original. He says

> The task of the translator consists in finding that intended effect upon the language into which he is translating which produces in it the echo of the original. . . . Unlike a work of literature, translation does not find itself in the center of the language forest but on the outside; it calls into it without entering, aiming at that single spot where the echo is able to give, in its own language, the reverberation of the work in the alien one.
>
> —W. Benjamin, "Die Aufgabe des Übersetzers,"
> originally a preface to Benjamin's translation
> of Baudelaire (Heidelberg, 1923), 77

I am never quite sure how to hear Sappho's echo but, now and again, reading these old citations, there is a tingle.

So far we have looked at examples of citation without context. Still more haunting are instances of context without citation. Some wonderful night of Sappho's life, not to say the prayer that it evoked, survives only as an allusion of the fourth-century-A.D. orator Libanius:

So if nothing prevented the Lesbian Sappho from praying that her night be made twice as long, let it be permitted me too to pray for something like this.

> —Libanius *Orations* 12.99 = Sappho fr. 197 Voigt

Some song of Sappho's that Solon heard sung by a boy is mentioned in an anecdote of Stobaios but Stobaios omits to tell us what song it was:

> Solon of Athens heard his nephew sing a song of Sappho's over the wine and since he liked the song so much he asked the boy to teach it to him. When someone asked why he said, *So that I may learn it then die.*

> —Stobaios *Florilegium* 3.29.58

Some shrewd thinking of Sappho's about death is paraphrased by Aristotle:

> Sappho says that to die is evil: so the gods judge. For they do not die.

> —Aristotle *Rhetoric* 1398b = Sappho fr. 201 Voigt

As acts of deterrence these stories carry their own kind of thrill—at the inside edge where her words go missing, a sort of antipoem that condenses everything you ever wanted her to write—but they cannot be called texts of Sappho's and so they are not included in this translation.

IF NOT, WINTER

Ποικιλόφροιν ἀθανάτ'Αφρόδιτα,
παῖ Διίος δολιόπλοκε, λίϛϛομαί ϛε,
μή μ'ι ἄϛαιϛι ιμηδ' ὀνίαιϛι δάμνα,
    πότνιια, θῦιμον,

ἀλλὰ τυίδ' ἔλιθ', αἴ ποτα κἀτέρωτα
τὰιϛ ἔμαϛ αὔιδαϛ ἀίοιϛα πήλοι
ἔκλυεϛ, πάτροιϛ δὲ δόμον λίποιϛα
    χιρύϛιον ἦλθιεϛ

ἄρμι' ὑπαϛδειύξαιϛα· κάλοι δέ ϛ' ἆγον
ὤικεεϛ ϛτροῦιθοι περὶ γᾶϛ μελαίναϛ
πύικνα δίνινεντεϛ πτέρ' ἀπ' ὠράνω αἴθε-
    ροιϛ διὰ μέϛϛω·

αἶιψα δ' ἐξίκοιντο· ϛὺ δ', ὦ μάκαιρα,
μειδιαίιϛαιϛ' ἀθανάτωι προϛώπωι
ἤιρε' ὄττιι δηῦτε πέπονθα κὤττι
    δηιῦτε κιάλιηιμμι

κιὤττι ιμοι μάλιϛτα θέλω γένεϛθαι
μιαινόλαι ιθύμωι· τίνα δηῦτε πείθω
ιϛάγην ιὲϛ ϛὰν φιλότατα; τίϛ ϛ', ὦ
    Ψάιπφ', ιἀδίκηιϛι;

Deathless Aphrodite of the spangled mind,
child of Zeus, who twists lures, I beg you
do not break with hard pains,
      O lady, my heart

but come here if ever before
you caught my voice far off
and listening left your father's
      golden house and came,

yoking your car. And fine birds brought you,
quick sparrows over the black earth
whipping their wings down the sky
      through midair—

they arrived. But you, O blessed one,
smiled in your deathless face
and asked what (now again) I have suffered and why
      (now again) I am calling out

and what I want to happen most of all
in my crazy heart. Whom should I persuade (now again)
to lead you back into her love? Who, O
      Sappho, is wronging you?

καὶ γὰρ αἰ φεύγει, ταχέως διώξει,
αἰ δὲ δῶρα μὴ δέκετ', ἀλλὰ δώϲει,
αἰ δὲ μὴ φίλει, ταχέως φιλήϲει
    κωὐκ ἐθέλοιϲα.

ἔλθε μοι καὶ νῦν, χαλέπαν δὲ λῦϲον
ἐκ μερίμναν, ὄϲϲα δέ μοι τέλεϲϲαι
θῦμοϲ ἰμέρρει, τέλεϲον, ϲὺ δ' αὔτα
    ϲύμμαχοϲ ἔϲϲο.

For if she flees, soon she will pursue.
If she refuses gifts, rather will she give them.
If she does not love, soon she will love
       even unwilling.

Come to me now: loose me from hard
care and all my heart longs
to accomplish, accomplish. You
       be my ally.

]
. . ανοθεν κατιου[ϲ]-
δευρυμμεκρητεϲιπ[.]ρ[   ]|. ναῦον
ἄγνον ὄππ[αι   ]| χάριεν μὲν ἄλϲος
μαλί[αν],| βῶμοι δ' ἔ‹ν›ι θυμιάμε—
      νοι [λι]|βανώτω‹ι›·

ἐν δ' ὔδωρ ψῦχροιν‹ι]| κελάδει δι' ὔϲδων
μαλίνων,| βρόδοιϲι δὲ παῖϲ ὀ χῶρος
ἐϲκίαϲτ', αἰθυϲϲομένων δὲ φύλλων|
      κῶμα καταιριον·

ἐν δὲ λείμων| ἰππόβοτος τέθαλε
τωτ. . .(.)ριν|νοις ἄνθεϲιν, αἰ ‹δ'› ἄηται
μέλλι|χα πν[έο]ιϲιν [
      [   ]

ἔνθα δὴ ϲὺ ϲυ.αν| ἔλοιϲα Κύπρι
χρυϲίαιϲιν ἐν κυλ|ίκεϲϲιν ἄβρως
‹ὀ›μ‹με›μεί|χμενον θαλίαιϲι| νέκταρ
      οἰνοχόειϲα

]
here to me from Krete to this holy temple
where is your graceful grove
of apple trees and altars smoking
       with frankincense.

And in it cold water makes a clear sound through
apple branches and with roses the whole place
is shadowed and down from radiant-shaking leaves
       sleep comes dropping.

And in it a horse meadow has come into bloom
with spring flowers and breezes
like honey are blowing
       [   ]

In this place you Kypris taking up
in gold cups delicately
nectar mingled with festivities:
       pour.

      ]δώϛην
κλ]ύτων μέντ᾽ ἐπ[
   κ]άλων κάϛλων, ϛ[
   ῾]λοις, λύπης τέμ[
]μ᾽ ὄνειδος
   ]οιδήϛαις . ἐπιτα[
]᾽αν, ἄϛαιο . τὸ γὰρ . [
]μον οὐκοῦτω μ[
] διάκηται,
   ]μηδ[   ] . αζε,
            ]χιϛ, ϛυνίημ[ι
         ] . ης κακότατο[ϛ
            ]μεν
            ]ν ἀτέραις με[
            ]η φρένας, εὔ[
            ]ατοις μακα[
               ]
                  ]α[

]to give

]yet of the glorious

]of the beautiful and good, you

      ]of pain   [me

]blame

]swollen

]you take your fill. For [my thinking

]not thus

]is arranged

]nor

all night long] I am aware

      ]of evildoing

      ]

      ]other

      ]minds

      ]blessed ones

      ]

      ]

]θε θῦμον

]μι πάμπαν

    ] δύναμαι,

    ]

]ας κεν ἦ μοι

]ϲαντιλάμπην

  ]λον πρόϲωπον.

  ]

  ]γχροΐϲθεις,

    ]΄[ ]ρος

]heart

]absolutely

]I can

]

]would be for me

]to shine in answer

]face

]

]having been stained

]

Κύπρι καὶ] Νηρήϊδες, ἀβλάβη[ν μοι
τὸν κασί]γνητον δ[ό]τε τυίδ᾽ ἴκεσθα[ι
κὤσσα Ϝ]οι θύμω‹ι› κε θέλη γένεσθαι
    πάντα τε]λέσθην,

ὄσσα δὲ πρ]όσθ᾽ ἄμβροτε πάντα λῦσα[ι
καὶ φίλοις]ι Ϝοῖα χάραν γένεσθαι
. . . . ἔ]χθροισι, γένοιτο δ᾽ ἄμμι
. . . . . . μ]ηδ᾽ εἶς·

τὰν κασιγ]νήταν δὲ θέλοι πόησθαι
    ]τίμας, [ὀν]ίαν δὲ λύγραν
    ]οτοισι π[ά]ροιθ᾽ ἀχεύων
    ].να
    ].εισαΐω[ν] τὸ κέγχρω
      ]λεπαγ[. . (´.)]αι πολίταν
      ]λλως[. . .]νηκε δ᾽ αὖτ᾽ οὐ
    ]κρω[ ]
    ]οναικ[ ]εο[ ].ι
    ]..[.]ν· σὺ [δ]ὲ Κύπ[ρι]..[..(.)]να
      ]θεμ[έν]α κάκαν [
    ]ι.

O Kypris and Nereids, undamaged I pray you
grant my brother to arrive here.
And all that in his heart he wants to be,
        make it be.

And all the wrong he did before, loose it.
Make him a joy to his friends,
a pain to his enemies and let there exist for us
        not one single further sorrow.

May he willingly give his sister
her portion of honor, but sad pain
                ]grieving for the past
                ]
                ]millet seed
                ]of the citizens
                ]once again no
                ]
                ]
                ]but you Kypris
                ]setting aside evil   [
                ]

ὠς δα.[
  κακκ[

ατρι[
κτα.[
.].[
  θα[

Cτείχ[
ὠς ἰδω[
τὰς ἐτ.[
  ποτνια.[

χρυcοπ[
καππο[
.ανμ[
  κᾶρα.[
  ].[

6

so

]

]

]

]

]

Go   [
so we may see [
]
lady

of gold arms [
]
]
doom
]

Δωρί]χας . [. . . . .] . [
    ]κην κέλετ᾽, οὐ γαρ [
    ]αις
    ]κάνην ἀγερωχία[
    ]μμεν᾽ ὄαν νέοιϲι[
    ] . αν φ[ι]λλ[. . . . .] . [
    ]μα . [

]Doricha's

]gives orders, for not

]

]top pride

]like young men

]beloved

]

].ν.ο.[

]αμφ.[

"Α]τθι· ϲο.[

].νέφ[

]   [

8

]
]
]Atthis for you
]
]

]αρκαλειοιτας ε̣.[

   ]παν οὐκεχη[

  ]ερ ἑόρταν

  ]μαν [Ἥ]ραι τελε[

    ]. ωνέμ[

     ].. ᾶς ἄ.[

      ]υςαι [

      ].ος δε[

      ]ν.[

]invites

]all not

]feast

]for Hera

]

]as long as

]

]

]

```
        ] . . . [
      ]ςθε . [
        ]        [
      ]νοημ[
   ] . απεδ[
   ΄] . ηνεο[
        ]        [
     ] . . ϱις . [
      ] . ιφ[
```

]
]
]
]thought
]barefoot
]
]
]
]

                              ]α μάκαι[ρ
                              ]ευπλο . [
                              ] ατοϲκα[
                              ]
]οϲθ[   ]βροτεκη[
 ]αταιϲ[   ]νεμ[
 ] . ύχαι λι . [   ]ενοϲ κλ[
    ] . [   ]

Κύ]πρι καί[ϲ]ε πι[κροτ΄ .]αν ἐπεύρ[οι
μη]δὲ καυχάϲ[α]ιτο τόδ᾽ ἐννέ[ποιϲα
Δ]ωρίχα τὸ δεύ[τ]ερον ὼϲ ποθε[
  ]ερον ἦλθε.

]blessed

]

]

]

to loose all the wrongs he did before

]

]by luck of the harbor

]

Kypris, and may she find you very bitter
and not go boasting—that Doricha—
how he came a second time
]to love's desire.

Ο]ἰ μὲν ἰππήων ϲτρότον, οἰ δὲ πέϲδων,
οἰ δὲ νάων φαῖϲ᾽ ἐπ[ὶ] γᾶν μέλαι[ν]αν
ἔ]μμεναι κάλλιϲτον, ἔγω δὲ κῆν᾽ ὄτ—
     τω τιϲ ἔραται·

πά]γχυ δ᾽ εὔμαρεϲ ϲύνετον πόηϲαι
π]άντι τ[ο]ῦτ᾽, ἀ γὰρ πόλυ περϲκέθοιϲα
κάλλοϲ [ἀνθ]ρώπων Ἐλένα [τὸ]ν ἄνδρα
     τὸν [αρ]ιϲτον

καλλ[ίποι]ϲ᾽ ἔβα ᾽ϲ Τροΐαν πλέοι[ϲα
κωὐδ[ὲ πα]ῖδοϲ οὐδὲ φίλων το[κ]ήων
πά[μπαν] ἐμνάϲθ‹η›, ἀλλὰ παράγαγ᾽ αὔταν
   `]ϲαν

      ]αμπτον γὰρ [
   ]...κούφωϲτ[   ]οη.[.]ν
..]με νῦν Ἀνακτορί[αϲ ὀ]νέμναι-
     ϲ᾽ οὐ] παρεοίϲαϲ,

Some men say an army of horse and some men say an army on foot
and some men say an army of ships is the most beautiful thing
on the black earth. But I say it is
      what you love.

Easy to make this understood by all.
For she who overcame everyone
in beauty (Helen)
      left her fine husband

behind and went sailing to Troy.
Not for her children nor her dear parents
had she a thought, no—
      ]led her astray

        ]for
        ]lightly
      ]reminded me now of Anaktoria
      who is gone.

τα]ς ‹κ›ε βολλοίμαν ἔρατόν τε βᾶμα
κἀμάρυχμα λάμπρον ἴδην προϲώπω
ἢ τὰ Λύδων ἄρματα κἀν ὄπλοιϲι
   πεϲδομ]άχενταϲ.

   ]. μεν οὐ δύνατον γένεϲθαι
   ]. ν ἀνθρωπ[. . (.) π]εδέχην δ᾽ ἄραϲθαι
[   ]
[   ]
[   ]
[   ]
[   ]

   προϲ[

   ὠϲδ[
   . .]. [
   .]. [.]ωλ. [
      τ᾽ ἐξ ἀδοκή[τω.

I would rather see her lovely step
and the motion of light on her face
than chariots of Lydians or ranks
    of footsoldiers in arms.

    ]not possible to happen
    ]to pray for a share
    ]
    ]
    ]
    ]
    ]
    toward[

    ]
    ]
    ]

    out of the unexpected.

Πλάςιον δη μ[
Πότνι᾽ ῞Ηρα ςὰ χ[
τὰν ἀράταν Ἀτ[ρέιδαι   κλῆ-]
    τοι βαςίληες·

ἐκτελέςςαντες μ[
πρῶτα μὲν περι.[
τυίδ᾽ ἀπορμάθεν[τες
    οὐκ ἐδύναντο

πρὶν ςὲ καὶ Δί᾽ ἀντ[
καὶ Θυώνας ἰμε[
νῦν δὲ κ[
    κὰτ τὸ παλ[

ἄγνα καὶ κα[
π]αρθ[εν
ἀ]μφι.[
    [   ]

[   ]
.[.].νιλ[
ἔμμενα[ι
    [?]ρ(᾽) ἀπίκε[ςθαι.

Close to me now as I pray,
lady Hera, may your gracious form appear,
to which the sons of Atreus prayed,
      glorious kings.

They won very many prizes
first at Troy then on the sea
and set out for here but
      could not complete the road

until they called on you and Zeus of suppliants
and Thyone's lovely child.
Now be gentle and help me too
      as of old[

Holy and beautiful
maiden
around[
      ]

]
]
to be
      ]to arrive.

⟨Π⟩άν κεδ[
⟨ἐ⟩ννέπην[
γλῶςςα μ[
    μυθολογη[

κἆνδρι . [
μεςδον[

Pan
to tell[
tongue[
     to tell tales[

and for a man
greater[

]
]μενοιϲα[
]θ' ἐν θύοιϲι[
] ἔχοιϲαν ἔϲλ[
]
]ει δὲ βαιϲα[
]ὺ γὰρ ἴδμεν[
]ιν ἔργων
]
]δ' ὐπίϲϲω [
κ]ἀπικυδ[
]τοδ' εἴπη[

]
]waiting
]in sacrifices
]having good
]
]but going
]for we know
]of works
]
]after
]and toward
]says this

]επι . ε_ςμα[

]ε, γάνος δὲ και . . [

]

τ]ύχαι ςὺν ἔςλαι

λί]μενος κρέτηςαι

γ]ᾶς μελαίνας

]

]έλοιςι ναῦται

] μεγάλαις ἀήται[ς

]α κἀπὶ χέρςω

]

']μοθεν πλέοι . [

]δε τὰ φόρτι' εἰκ[

]νατιμ' ἐπεὶ κ . [

]

]ρέοντι πόλλ . . [

]αιδέκα[

]ει

]

]ιν ἔργα

] χέρςω [

] . α

]

'] . . [

]
]gladness and
]
]with good luck
]to gain the harbor
]of black earth
]
]sailors
]in big blasts of wind
]upon dry land
]
]sail
]the freight
]when
]
]many
]
]
]
]works
]dry land
]
]
]

      ]

      ].επαβοληϲ[

      ]ανδ' ὄλοφυν [. . . .]ε.

      ] τρομέροιϲ π.[. .]ᾳλλα

      ]

        ] χρόα γῆραϲ ἤδη

          ]ν ἀμφιβάϲκει

            ]ϲ πέταται διώκων

            ]

            ]ταϲ ἀγαύαϲ

          ]ε̣α, λάβοιϲα

          ]ι̯ᾰ̈ειϲον ἄμμι

⌞τὰν ἰόκολπον⌟   ]

                ]ρων μάλιϲτα

                  ]αϲ π[λ]άναται

   ]

   ]

   ]pity

   ]trembling

   ]

   ]flesh by now old age

   ]covers

   ]flies in pursuit

   ]

   ]noble

   ]taking

   ]sing to us

the one with violets in her lap

   ]mostly

   ]goes astray

]βλα.[

]εργον, . .λ᾽α. .[

]ν ῥέθος δοκιμ[

]ηϲθαι

]ν αὐάδην χ.[

δ]ὲ μή, χείμων[

].οιϲαναλγεα.[

]δε

.].ε.[. . .].[. . κ]έλομαι ϲ.[

. .].γυλα.[. . .]ανθι λάβοιϲα.α.[

πᾶ]κτιν, ἆς ϲε δηῦτε πόθος τ.[

ἀμφιπόταται

τὰν κάλαν· ἀ γὰρ κατάγωγις αὔτα[

ἐπτόαις᾽ ἴδοιϲαν, ἔγω δὲ χαίρω,

καὶ γὰρ αὔτα δή πο[τ᾽] ἐμεμφ[

Κ]υπρογέν[ηα

ὠς ἄραμα[ι

τοῦτο τῶ[

β]όλλομα[ι

```
        ]
        ]work
        ]face
        ]
        ]
        if not, winter
        ]no pain
        ]
]I bid you sing
of Gongyla, Abanthis, taking up
your lyre as (now again) longing
        floats around you,


you beauty. For her dress when you saw it
stirred you. And I rejoice.
In fact she herself once blamed me
        Kyprogeneia


because I prayed
this word:
I want
```

]ἔρωτος ἠλπ[

]

αν]τιον εἰϲίδωϲ[

] Ἐρμιόνα τεαυ[τα

] ξάνθαι δ' Ἐλέναι ϲ' εἰϲ[κ]ην

]κεϲ

].ιϲ θνάταιϲ, τόδε δ' ἴϲ[θι,] τὰι ϲᾶι

]παίϲαν κέ με τὰν μερίμναν

]λαιϲ' ἀντιδ[..]'[.]αθοιϲ δὲ

]

]ταϲ ὄχθοιϲ

]ταιν

παν]νυχίϲ[δ]ην

] [

]of desire

]

]for when I look at you

]such a Hermione

]and to yellowhaired Helen I liken you

]

]among mortal women, know this

]from every care

]you could release me

]

]dewy riverbanks

]to last all night long

] [

]ανάγα[

].[ ]εμνάϲεϲθ' ἀ[
κ]αὶ γὰρ ἄμμεϲ ἐν νεό[τατι
ταῦτ' [ἐ]πόημμεν·

πόλλα [μ]ὲν γὰρ καὶ κά[λα
...η.[ ]μεν, πολι[
.μμε[.]ο[.]είαιϲ δ[
.].[.]..[

]νθα[
ζ]ώομ[εν
]ω· ν..[
]εναντ[
]απάππ[
τ]όλμαν[
]ανθρω[
.]ονεχ[
]παιϲα[

24A

]
]you will remember
]for we in our youth
        did these things

yes many and beautiful things
]
]
        ]

24C

]
]we live
]
the opposite
]
daring
]
]
]

].έδαφο[
]αικατε[
]ανέλο[
]
  ]. [   ]. αι
λ]επτοφών[
  ]. εα. [

]

]

]

]

]

]in a thin voice

]

]γμε . [

]προλιπ[

]νυᾶϲεπ[

ἄ]βρα·

ἐ]γλάθαν' ἐϲ[

   ]ηϲμεθα[

]γυνθαλα[

]
]quit
]
]luxurious woman
]
]
]

]θαμέω[

ὄ‚ττιναις γὰρ

εὖ θέω, κῆνοί με μά‚λιςτα πά[ντων

ςίνονται‚

        ] ἀλεμάτ[

        ] . γονωμ[

        ] . ιμ᾽ οὐ πρ[

        ]αι

        ] ςέ, θέλω[

        ]το πάθη[

        ] . αν, ἔγω δ᾽ ἔμ᾽ ιαῦται

τοῦτο ςύ‚νοιδα

        ] . [.] . τοις[. . .] . [

        ]εναμ[

        ] . [.] . [

26

        ]frequently

        ]for those

I treat well are the ones who most of all

        ]harm me

            ]crazy

            ]

            ]

            ]

            ]you, I want

            ]to suffer

        ]in myself I am

aware of this

]

]

]

                    ]καιπ[
              ] . [.] . [.]γος[
              ]ςι·
...] . καὶ γὰρ δὴ ςὺ πάις ποτ[
...]ικης μέλπεςθ' ἄγι ταῦτα[
..] ζάλεξαι, κάμμ' ἀπὺ τωδεκ[
     ἄ]δρα χάριςςαι·

ς]τείχομεν γὰρ ἐς γάμον· εὖ δε[
κα]ὶ ςὺ τοῦτ', ἀλλ' ὅττι τάχιςτα[
πα]ρ[θ]ένοις ἄπ[π]εμπε, θέοι[
     ]εν ἔχοιεν

        ] ὄδος μ[έ]γαν εἰς Ὄλ[υμπον
          ἀ]νθρωπ   ]αίκ . [

]

]

]

]yes you a child once
]come sing these things
]talk to us, give us your
       grace

for we go to a wedding: and surely
you know this, but as soon as possible
send the girls away, may gods
       have

]road to great Olympos
]for men

] . ιων[
]μέτριακα[
β]άθυ δου . [
]αν[

]

]ανταμε[
] . ι πότνια[
]αψατ[
]ον

29A

]
]
deep sound
]

29B

]

]
lady
]
]

]πεπλ[
].ι[.]ορμοις[.]τε[
].[...].[.]ω

].α[...].[..]αποι[
].ω[....]τ[
].ιγο[...]..[......].[
].

].[.]λμ[   ].[.].[
]ντε Γόργοι .[.].[
]δε· [   ]..[..].[
].μ.[

]robes

]necklaces

]

]

]

]

]

]

]for Gorgo

]

]

] [

]̣ οιϲα[.̣].̣
Γ]ύριννοι
]̣ αυταν
]

]ϛ΄ ἔοιϲαν
]λοιϲα
].̣[

]

]

for Gyrinno

]

]

]

]

]

νύκτ[. . .]. [

πάρθενοι δ[
παννυχίςδοι[ς]αι[
ςὰν ἀείδοις[ι]ν φ[ιλότατα καὶ νύμ—
    φας ἰοκόλπω.

ἀλλ' ἐγέρθεις, ἠϊθ[ε
ςτεῖχε ςοὶς ὐμάλικ[ας
ἤπερ ὄςςον ἀ λιγύφω[νος
    ὔπνον [ἴ]δωμεν.

night[

girls
all night long
might sing of the love between you and the bride
        with violets in her lap

wake! and go call
the young men so that
no more than the bird with piercing voice
        shall we sleep

Φαίνεταί μοι κῆνος ἴςος θέοιςιν
ἔμμεν' ὤνηρ, ὄττις ἐνάντιός τοι
ἰςδάνει καὶ πλάςιον ἆδυ φωνεί-
        ςας ὑπακούει

καὶ γελαίςας ἰμέροεν, τό μ' ἦ μὰν
καρδίαν ἐν ςτήθεςιν ἐπτόαιςεν·
ὡς γὰρ <ἔς> ς' ἴδω βρόχε' ὥς με φώνη-
        ς' οὐδὲν ἔτ' εἴκει,

ἀλλὰ καμ μὲν γλῶςςα ἔαγε, λέπτον
δ' αὔτικα χρῶι πῦρ ὑπαδεδρόμακεν,
ὀππάτεςςι δ' οὐδὲν ὄρημμ', ἐπιβρό-
        μειςι δ' ἄκουαι,

ἔκαδε μ' ἴδρως κακχέεται, τρόμος δὲ
παῖςαν ἄγρει, χλωροτιέρα δὲ πιοίας
ἔμμι, τεθινάκην δ' ὀλίγω 'πιδειύης
        φαμίνομ' ἔμ' αὔτ[αι.

ἀλλὰ πὰν τόλματον, ἐπεὶ καὶ πένητα

He seems to me equal to gods that man
whoever he is who opposite you
sits and listens close
       to your sweet speaking

and lovely laughing—oh it
puts the heart in my chest on wings
for when I look at you, even a moment, no speaking
       is left in me

no: tongue breaks and thin
fire is racing under skin
and in eyes no sight and drumming
       fills ears

and cold sweat holds me and shaking
grips me all, greener than grass
I am and dead—or almost
       I seem to me.

But all is to be dared, because even a person of poverty

αἴ με τιμίαν ἐπόησαν ἔργα
τὰ ϲφὰ δοῖϲαι

who honored me
by giving their works

αἴθ' ἔγω, χρυϲοϲτέφαν' Ἀφρόδιτα,
τόνδε τὸν πάλον λαχοίην

if only I, O goldcrowned Aphrodite,

could win this lot

ἄϲτερεϲ μὲν ἀμφὶ κάλαν ϲελάνναν
ἂψ ἀπυκρύπτοιϲι φάεννον εἶδος
ὄπποτα πλήθοιϲα μάλιϲτα λάμπη
   γᾶν

         ἀργυρία

stars around the beautiful moon

hide back their luminous form

whenever all full she shines
         on the earth

         silvery

ἤ σε Κύπρος ἢ Πάφος ἢ Πάνορμος

you either Kypros or Paphos or Panormos

καὶ ποθήω καὶ μάομαι

I long and seek after

κὰτ ἔμον ϛτάλυγμον

τὸν δ' ἐπιπλάζοντ' ἄνεμοι φέροιεν
καὶ μελέδωναι

in my dripping (pain)

the blamer may winds and terrors
carry him off

ὄπταις ἄμμε

you burn me

πόδα‹ς› δὲ
ποίκιλος μάςλης ἐκάλυπτε, Λύδι-
ον κάλον ἔργον

                    the feet
by spangled straps covered
beautiful Lydian work

ϲοὶ δ' ἔγω λεύκαϲ επιδωμον αἶγοϲ

κἀπιλείψω τοι

but I to you of a white goat

and I will pour wine over

ταὶς κάλαις· ὔμμιν ‹τὸ› νόημμα τὦμον
οὐ διάμειπτον

for you beautiful ones my thought
is not changeable

ταῖα ψῦχρος μὲν ἔγεντο θῦμος
πὰρ δ' ἴεισι τὰ πτέρα

42

their heart grew cold
they let their wings down

]αι·

]

]λεται

] ⟦κ⟧αλος

]. ἄκαλα κλόνει

] κάματος φρένα

]ε κατισδάνε[ι]

] ἀλλ' ἄγιτ', ὦ φίλαι,

], ἄγχι γὰρ ἀμέρα.

]
]
]
]beautiful he
]stirs up still things
]exhaustion the mind
]settles down
]but come O beloveds
]for day is near

Κυπρο.[   ]ας·
κᾶρυξ ἦλθε θε[   ]ελε[...].θεις
Ἴδαος ταδεκα...φ[..].ις τάχυς ἄγγελος

τάς τ' ἄλλας Ἀςίας .[.]δε.αν κλέος ἄφθιτον·
Ἕκτωρ καὶ ςυνέταιρ[ο]ι ἄγοις' ἐλικώπιδα
Θήβας ἐξ ἱέρας Πλακίας τ' ἀπ' [ἀϊ]ν‹ν›άω
ἄβραν Ἀνδρομάχαν ἐνὶ ναῦςιν ἐπ' ἄλμυρον
πόντον· πόλλα δ' [ἐλί]γματα χρύςια κἄμματα
πορφύρ[α] καταΰτ[με]να, ποίκιλ' ἀθύρματα,
ἀργύρα τ' ἀνάρι..θμα ιποτή.ρια. κάλέφαις.
ὢς εἶπ· ὀτραλέως δ' ἀνόρουςε πάτ[η]ρ φίλος·
φάμα δ' ἦλθε κατὰ πτόλιν εὐρύχορον φίλοις.
αὖτικ' Ἰλίαδαι ςατίναι[ς] ὐπ' ἐυτρόχοις
ἆγον αἰμιόνοις, ἐπ[έ]βαινε δὲ παῖς ὄχλος
γυναίκων τ' ἄμα παρθενίκα[ν] τ..[..].ςφύρων,
χῶρις δ' αὖ Περάμοιο θυγα[α]τρες[
ἵππ[οις] δ' ἄνδρες ὔπαγον ὐπ' ἄρ[ματα
π[   ]ες ἠίθεοι, μεγάλω[ς]τι δ[
δ[   ]. ἀνίοχοι φ[.....].[
π[']ξα.ο[

Kypros

herald came

Idaos   swift messenger

]

and of the rest of Asia   imperishable fame.

Hektor and his men are bringing a glancing girl

from holy Thebe and from onflowing Plakia—

delicate Andromache on ships over the salt

sea. And many gold bracelets and purple

perfumed clothes, painted toys,

and silver cups innumerable and ivory.

So he spoke. And at once the dear father rose up.

And news went through the wide town to friends.

Then sons of Ilos led mules beneath

fine-running carts and up climbed a whole crowd

of women and maidens with tapering ankles,

but separately the daughters of Priam   [

And young men led horses under chariots   [

]in great style

]charioteers

]

                                        ἴ]κελοι θέοι[ς
                                        ] ἄγνον ἀολ[λε
ι̯ὄρμαται̯·[   ]νον ἐς Ἴλιο[ν
ι̯αῦλος δ' ἀδυ[μ]έλης·[   ]τ' ὀνεμίγνυ[το
ι̯καὶ ψ[ό]ψο[ς κ]ροτάλ·[ων   ]ως δ' ἄρα πάρ[θενοι
ι̯ἄειδον μέλος ἄγγ·[ον, ἴκα]νε δ' ἐς αἴθ[ερα
ι̯ἄχω θεσπεσία γελ·[
ι̯πάνται δ' ἦς κὰτ ὄδο·[ις
ι̯κράτηρες·| φίαλαί τ' ὀ·[. . .]υεδε[. .] . εακ[.] . [
ι̯μύρρα καὶ κασία λίβ·ανός τ' ὀνεμείχνυτο
ι̯γύναικες δ' ἐλέλυς·δο·ν ὄσαι προγενέστερα[ι
ι̯πάντες δ' ἄνδρες ἐπ·ήρατον ἴαχον ὄρθιον
ι̯πάον' ὀνκαλέοντες·| Ἐκάβολον εὐλύραν
ι̯ὔμνην δ' Ἔκτορα κ' Ἀν·δρομάχαν θεο‹ε›ικέλο[ις.

                              ]like to gods
                              ]holy all together
set out   for Ilios
and sweetflowing flute and kithara were mingled
with the clip of castanets and piercingly then the maidens
sang a holy song and straight up the air went
amazing sound   [
and everywhere in the roads was [
bowls and cups   [
myrrh and cassia and frankincense were mingled.
And all the elder women shouted aloud
and all the men cried out a lovely song
calling on Paon farshooting god of the lyre,
and they were singing a hymn for Hektor and Andromache
   like to gods.

]ϲανορεϲ . . [

Φοίβωι χρυϲοκό]μαι τὸν ἔτικτε Κόω . [

μίγειϲ(α)   Κρ]ονίδαι μεγαλωνύμῳ‹ι›.

Ἄρτεμιϲ δὲ θέων] μέγαν ὄρκον ἀπώμοϲε

     κεφά]λαν· ἄϊ πάρθενος ἔϲϲομαι

      ] . ων ὀρέων κορύφαιϲ᾽ ἔπι

        ]δε νεῦϲον ἔμαν χάριν·

      ἔνευ]ϲε θέων μακάρων πάτηρ·

     ἐλαφάβ]ολον ἀγροτέραν θέοι

       ] . ϲιν ἐπωνύμιον μέγα·

        ]ερος οὐδάμα πίλναται·

          ] . [.] . . . μαφόβε[. .]έρω·

ἔμμ[

και . [

ρ . ε . [

ω . . . [

Μοιϲαν ἀγλα[

πόει καὶ Χαρίτων [

βραδίνοιϲ ἐπεβ . [

ὄργας μὴ ᾽πιλάθε . [

θγάτοιϲιν· πεδ᾽ χ[

       ]δαλίω[

]

for goldhaired Phoibos whom Koos' daughter bore

after she mingled with Kronos' highnamed son.

But Artemis swore the great oath of the gods:

By your head! forever virgin shall I be

]untamed on solitary mountains

]Come, nod yes to this for my sake!

So she spoke. Then the father of blessed gods nodded yes.

Virgin deershooter wild one the gods

call her as her name.

]Eros comes nowhere near her

]

44AB

              [

              [

              [

              [

of the Muses   [

makes and of the Graces [

with slender

              [

for mortals: there is a share [

]

ᾶς θέλετ' ὔμμες

45

as long as you want

ἔγω δ' ἐπὶ μολθάκαν
τύλαν ‹κα›ϲπολέω μέλεα· κἂν μὲν τετύλαγκαϲ ἀϲπόλεα

and I on a soft pillow
will lay down my limbs

Ἔρος δ' ἐτίναξέ ⟨μοι⟩
φρένας, ὡς ἄνεμος κὰτ ὄρος δρύςιν ἐμπέτων

Eros shook my

mind like a mountain wind falling on oak trees

ἦλθες ἔγω δέ ς' ἐμαιόμαν,
ὂν δ' ἔψυξας ἔμαν φρένα καιομέναν πόθωι

you came and I was crazy for you
and you cooled my mind that burned with longing

Ἠράμαν μὲν ἔγω ϲέθεν, Ἄτθι, πάλαι ποτά

ϲμίκρα μοι πάις ἔμμεν᾽ ἐφαίνεο κἄχαρις

I loved you, Atthis, once long ago

a little child you seemed to me and graceless

ὀ μὲν γὰρ κάλος ὄςςον ἴδην πέλεται ‹κάλος›,
ὀ δὲ κἄγαθος αὔτικα καὶ κάλος ἔς‹ςε›ται.

For the man who is beautiful is beautiful to see

but the good man will at once also beautiful be.

οὐκ οἶδ᾽ ὄττι θέω· δύο μοι τὰ νοήματα

51

I don't know what to do

two states of mind in me

ψαύην δ' οὐ δοκίμωμ' ὀράνω δυσπαχέα

I would not think to touch the sky with two arms

Βροδοπάχεες ἄγναι Χάριτες, δεῦτε Δίος κόραι

pure Graces with arms like roses

come here daughters of Zeus

ἔλθοντ᾽ ἐξ ὀράνω πορφυρίαν περθέμενον χλάμυν

having come from heaven wrapped in a purple cloak

κατθάνοιϲα δὲ κείϲηι οὐδέ ποτα μναμοϲύνα ϲέθεν
ἔϲϲετ' οὐδὲ ποκ' ὕϲτερον· οὐ γὰρ πεδέχηις βρόδων
τὼν ἐκ Πιερίας, ἀλλ' ἀφάνης κἀν Ἀίδα δόμωι
φοιτάϲηις πεδ' ἀμαύρων νεκύων ἐκπεποταμένα.

Dead you will lie and never memory of you

will there be nor desire into the aftertime—for you do not

   share in the roses

of Pieria, but invisible too in Hades' house

you will go your way among dim shapes. Having been breathed out.

οὐδ' ἴαν δοκίμωμι προςίδοιςαν φάος ἀλίω
ἔςςεςθαι ςοφίαν πάρθενον εἰς οὐδένα πω χρόνον
τεαύταν

not one girl I think
    who looks on the light of the sun
        will ever
        have wisdom
        like this

τίς δ' ἀγροΐωτις θέλγει νόον
ἀγροΐωτιν ἐπεμμένα ςτόλαν
οὐκ ἐπιςταμένα τὰ βράκε' ἔλκην ἐπὶ τῶν ςφύρων;

what country girl seduces your wits

wearing a country dress

not knowing how to pull the cloth to her ankles?

].[

]. δα[

]

]. α

]ύγοιϲα[ ]

].[..].. [   ]ιδάχθην

]χυ θ[.']ρι[.]αλλ[.......]ύταν

]. χθο.[.]ατί.[.....]ειϲα

]μένα ταν[....ώ]νυμόν ϲε

]νι θῆται ϲτ[ύ]μα[τι] πρόκοψιν

]πων κάλα δῶρα παῖδες

.]φιλάοιδον λιγύραν χελύνναν

πά]ντα χρόα γῆρας ἤδη

λεῦκαί τ᾽ ἐγένο]ντο τρίχες ἐκ μελαίναν

]αι, γόνα δ᾽ [ο]ὐ φέροιϲι

]ηϲθ᾽ ἴϲα νεβρίοιϲιν

ἀ]λλὰ τί κεν ποείην;

] οὐ δύνατον γένεϲθαι

] βροδόπαχυν Αὔων

ἔϲ]χατα γᾶς φέροιϲα[

]ον ὔμως ἔμαρψε[

]άταν ἄκοιτιν

]ιμέναν νομίϲδει

]αις ὀπάϲδοι

ι̇ἔγω δὲ φίλημμ᾽ ἀβροϲύναν,˩   ] τοῦτο καί μοι
τὸ λάι̇μπρον ἔρως ἀελίω καὶ τὸ κάι̇λον λέι̇λˌογχε.

]

]

]

]

]running away

]bitten

]

]

]you

]makes a way with the mouth

]beautiful gifts children

]songdelighting clearsounding lyre

]all my skin old age already

hair turned white after black

]knees do not carry

]like fawns

]but what could I do?

]not possible to become

]Dawn with arms of roses

]bringing to the ends of the earth

]yet seized

]wife

]imagines

]might bestow

But I love delicacy   and this to me—
the brilliance and beauty of the sun—desire has allotted.

'Επιν[   ].[. . .]γό.[
φίλει.[

καιν[

59

]
loves

new

]τύχοισα
] θέλ᾽ ωνταπαίϲαν
τέ]λεϲον νόημμα
]έτων κάλημι
] πεδὰ θῦμον αἶψα
ὄ]ϲϲα τύχην θελήϲη[ϲ
]ϱ ἔμοι μάχεϲθα[ι
χ]λιδάνα‹ι› πίθειϲα[
]ι, ϲὺ δ᾽ εὖ γὰϱ οἶϲθα
]έτει τα[.].λε..
]κλαϲ[

]having encountered

]wants

]accomplish the plan

]I call out

]to the heart at once

]all that you wish to win

]to fight for me

]by the wanton one persuaded

]but yes you know well

]

]

ἔγεντ.[
οὐ γάρ κ[ε

61

they became [
for not

Ἐπτάξατε̣[
δάφνας ὄτα[

πὰν δ' ἄδιον[
ἢ κῆνον ἐλο[

καὶ ταῖϲι μὲν ἀ̣[
ὀδοίποροϲ ἄν[. . . .] . . [

μύγις δέ ποτ' εἰϲάιον· ἐκλ[
ψύχα δ' ἀγαπάταϲυ . [΄

τέαυτα δὲ νῦν ἔμμ[
ἴκεϲθ' ἀγανα[

ἔφθατε· κάλαν[
τά τ' ἔμματα κα[

You cowered   [
laurel tree   [

but everything sweeter   [
than that   [

and for them   [
traveler   [

But I scarcely ever listened   [
soul beloved   [

and such now   [
to arrive kindly   [

You got there first: beautiful   [
and the clothes   [

Ὄνοιρε μελαινα[
φ[ο]ίταις, ὄτα τ' ὔπνος [

γλύκυς θ[έ]ος, ἦ δεῖν' ὀνίας μ[
ζὰ χῶρις ἔχην τὰν δυναμ[

ἔλπις δέ μ' ἔχει μὴ πεδέχη[ν
μηδὲν μακάρων ἐλ[

οὐ γάρ κ' ἔον οὔτω[΄
ἀθύρματα κα.[

γένοιτο δέ μοι[
τοὶς πάντα[

dream of black   [
you come roaming and when sleep   [

sweet god, terribly from pain   [
to hold the strength separate   [

but I expect not to share   [
nothing of the blessed ones   [

for I would not be like this   [
toys   [

but may it happen to me   [
all   [

]λακ[

]

]νί . [

α]λίκεϲαι[

]

]παίδων[

]δηον

]

]

]θεντ[

] . θέοιϲ[

]ν αἴϲχρ[

]

]α μοῖ[

]τετι[

] . α[

]αίγα[

] . δο . [

] [. [

]
]
]   goat
]for comrades
]
]of children
]
]
]
]
]to gods
]ugly
]
]Muse
]

.....].. . α[
.....]ϱομε[
.....]. ελας[
. ϱοτήννεμε[
Ψάπφοι, ςεφίλ[
Κύπϱωι β[α]ςίλ[
χαίτοι μέγα δ. [
ὄ]ςςοις φαέθων [
πάνται κλέος [

καί ς᾽ ἐνν Ἀχέϱ[οντ
..[.....]γπ[

65

]
]
]
]
to Sappho, you   [
in Kypros queen   [
and yet greatly   [
to all on whom the blazing   [
everywhere glory   [

and you in Acheron's
]

67A

. .]ων μα.[

κ]αὶ τοῦτ' ἐπικε.[
δ]αίμων ὀλοφ.[

οὐ μὰν ἐφίλης[
νῦν δ' ἔννεκα[

τὸ δ' αἴτιον οὐτ[
ῥὐδὲν πόλυ[.].[

.]υδ' ["

67B

].ουδε[
]ταυτα.[
]λαιϛιμ[
]πλήονι[
]' ἀμφ[
].ϛθεο.[
]έρως.[

67A

]

and this   [
ruinous god   [

I swear did not love   [
but now because   [

and the reason neither   [
nothing much   [

                            [

67B

]nor
]these
]
]more
]around
]
]desire

]ι̣ γάρ μ' ἀπὺ τὰς ἐ.[
     ὔ]μως δ' ἔγεν[το
       ] ἴϲαν θέοιϲιν
    ]αϲαν ἀλίτρα[
   Ἀν]δρομέδαν[.].αξ[
   ]αρ[...].α μάκα[ιρ]α
  ]ϱον δὲ τρόπον α[.].ύνη[
    ] κόρον οὐ κατιϲχε.[
]κα[.....]. Τυνδαρίδαι[ϲ
]αϲυ[.]...κα[.] χαρίεντ' ἀ.[
]κ' ἄδολον [μ]ηκέτι ϲυν[
] Μεγάρα.[..]να[...]α[

    ]....φ[
  ].[.]'θύρα.[
 ]μοι χάλε.[
   ]δεκύ[
    ]. οπάλην ὄλ[
    ]ε[

]for me away from
      ]yet turned out to be
      ]her like gods
            ]sinful
            ]Andromeda
                  ]blessed one
            ]way
            ]did not restrain excess
            ]Tyndarids
            ]gracious
]innocent no longer
]Megara

            ]
            ]playing
            ]for me harsh
            ]
            ]
            ]

]ε . . [.]τεγαμ[
]ας ἀλίτρα[
          ]έτ᾿ αὐ[

]
]sinful
]

]αμ. λ. [
]ναμ[
]γ δ' εἶμ' ε[
]ρϲομέν[
]λικ' ὐπα[
] . . . [.]βα[
]ϲ γὰρ ἐπαυ[
] μάν κ' ἀπυθυϲ[
]αρμονίαϲ δ[
]αθην χόρον, ἄα[
]δε λίγηα. [
]ατόν ϲφι[
] πάντεϲϲι[
]επ[.] . [

]
]
]I will go
]
]
]
]for
]
]of Harmonia
]dance
]clearsounding
]
]to all
]

]μισσε Μίκα

]ελα[. .ἀλ]λά ς' ἔγωὐκ
ἐάςω

]ν φιλότ[ατ'] ἤλεο Πενθιλήαν[

]δα κα[κό]τροπ', ἄμμα[

] μέλ[ος] τι γλύκερον .[

]α μελλιχόφων[ος

]δει, λίγυραι δ' ἄη[

] δρος[ό]εσσα[

]you Mika

]but I will not allow you

]you chose the love of Penthelids

]evilturning

]some sweet song

]in honey voice

]piercing breezes

]wet with dew

]νβ.[.].[.]υ
]α
]αν 'Αφροδι[τα
ἀ]δύλογοι δ' ἐρ[
]βαλλοι
α]ις ἔχοισα
].ένα θααϛ[ϛ
]άλλει
]αϛ ἐέρϛαϛ [

]

]

]Aphrodite

]sweetworded desires

]throw

]holding

]sits

]

]dews

74A	74B	74C

]ων ἔκα[

]αιπόλ[

]μ.[

]βροδο[

]ρνθ[

]φαιμ[

]α[

]ποθρ[

].ὠβα[

].[

]ας ἴδρω[

].υζαδ.[

]ιν[

74A   74B   74C

]   ]   ]
]goatherd   ]longing   ]sweat
]   ]   ]
]roses   ]
]
]

]αγ πα[
τε]λέϲειε κ[
]ίη λελα[
]ε θέλω[
]εχην[
]η· ἔφα.[
]αλίκ[

]
]might accomplish
]
]I want
]to hold
]said
]

].οναυ[

]ην οὐδε[

　]ης ἴμερ[

].αι δ' ἄμα[

].ανθος·[

　ἴ]μερον[

　]ετερπ[

]
]nor
]desire
]but all at once
]blossom
]desire
]took delight

].[
].τοϲεϲ.[
]παντα[
]ι δ' ἀτέρα[
]λοκα[
].[

]
]
]all
]but different
]hair
]

]απύθες.[
]χιϲταλ[
]εμπ[

ϲὺ δὲ ϲτεφάνοις, ὦ Δίκα, πⅼέρθεϲιθ' ἐράτοις φόβαιϲιν
ὄρπακας ἀνήτω ϲυν‹α›ⅼεⅰρρⅼαιϲⅰ' ἀπάλαιϲι χέρϲιν·
εὐάνθεα γὰρ πέλεται καὶ Χάριτες μάκαιρα‹ι›
μᾶλλον προτερην, ἀϲτεφανώτοιϲι δ' ἀπυϲτρέφονται.

]despise

]quick as possible

]

But you, O Dika, bind your hair with lovely crowns,

tying stems of anise together in your soft hands.

For the blessed Graces prefer to look on one who wears flowers

and turn away from those without a crown.

82A

Εὐμορφοτέρα Μνασιδίκα τὰς ἀπάλας Γυρίννως

82B

καίτ᾿ ἐ[
μηδεν[

νῦν δ᾿ ἀ[
μὴ βόλλῃ[

εὐ]μορφο[τέρα

82A

Mnasidika more finely shaped than soft Gyrinno

82B

and if   [
nothing   [

but now   [
don't   [

more finely shaped

].αί.[
]λ' αὖθι με[
]νώμεθ' ὀ[
] δηῦτ' ἐπιτ[
]έντηδεμ[
].α γὰρ ἐκά[
].[.].[

]
]right here
]
](now again)
]
]for
]

]․αις[
]․ικιπ[
]ων κ[․․]․[․?]ίνα[
]τονόνε․[․?]․οϛε[
]άβροις ἐπιχ[?]ημ[
]αν Ἀρτεμι[
]ναβλ[

]
]
]
]reproach
]delicate
]Artemis
]

]..

ʼ]λβον

]ακούην

]αύταν

]πάμεν̣α[

]τʼ ὦϲτʼ ὸ πέλη[

]ακαν ϲό[

85A   85B

]   ]
]prosperous   ]like an old man
]to listen   ]
]

].ακάλα.[

] αἰγιόχω λα[

]. Κυθέρη᾽ εὔχομ[

   ]ον ἔχοισα θῦμο[ν

κλ]ῦθί μ᾽ ἄρας αἴ π[οτα κἀτέρωτα

   ]ας προλίποισα κ[

   ]. πεδ᾽ ἔμαν ἰώ[

     ].ν χαλέπαι.[

]quiet

]with an aegis

]Kytherea I pray

]holding the heart

]hear my prayer if ever at other times

]forsaking

]toward my

]harsh

]αμμ[

]ικα. [

]ποίϲαι[

]κλεηδον[

]. πλοκαμ[

]εϲδ' ἀμα[

] ἀνθρώπ[

]. υμαιν[

]τεκαιπ[

μ]εριμνα[

]γην [

]αικο[

]αι   [

[.]δω.[

τόλμ[

87A

]
]
]
]rumor
]hair
]at the same time
]man
]
]

87B

]anxiety
]ground
]
]

87C

]
]daring

            ]

        ]

]εϛθα

]ρπον ἄβαν

]

]εϛθαι·

]

].

]

]

]

]

]

] youth

]

]

]

]

]

]

]εφι.[
β]ασιλη.[
]εγαδ.[
].ος.[

΄]δη[
΄]κωσα[
]ν· σοι[
].δηκ.[
]εςιππ[
].αλ.[
].εςσα[
].[.].[

87E

]
]queen
]
]

87F

]
]
]to you
]
]horse
]
]
]

]̣[

]ν προ̣..[
]νως πρὸς πότ[
].ατον χάλα[

].θέλοις· οὐδυ[
].αςδοις' ὀλιγα[
].ένα φέρεςθα[ι

].φιạ τις...[

ἐμ[   ].δ' ἄδιον εἰςορ[
τρῦ[ο]ἶϲθα καὔτα·

κ[λέ]λαθ' ἀλλονιά[
ςε[   ].αν· τιραδ[
ἠ[   ]αί τις εἴποι

ἀ[   ].ςαν· ἔγω τε γαρ[
φιλη[   ]μ' ᾶς κεν ἔνη μ'[
κᾶλ.[   ]αι μελήςην·

ἐςτ.[   ]φίλα φαῖμ' ἐχύρα γέ[νεςθαι
.]χα[   ]ενα[.]αις· ἀτ[
]..δ' ὀνίαρ[ο]ς [

]

]in front
]toward
]loosen

]you would be willing
]slight
]to be carried

]someone
]me   ]more sweetly
]   ]and you yourself know

]   ]forgot
]you   ]
]   ]someone would say

]   ]and yes I
shall love   ]as long as there is in me
]   ]will be a care

]   ]I say I have been a strong lover
]   ]

]painful

].πίκρος ὔμ[

].[.]τα.θᾶδ[

].α τόδε δ' ἴς[θ(ι)

].ὤττι ς' ἐ.[

  ]α φιλήςω[

  ]τω τι λο[

  ]ςςον γὰρ .[

]ςθαι βελέω[ν

]..[

]bitter
]
]and know this

]whatever you
]I shall love
]

]for
]of weapons
]

ἀϲαροτέραϲ οὐδάμα πω Εἴρανα, ϲέθεν τύχοιϲαν

never more damaging O Eirana have I encountered you

[

[

πε[

κρ[. . . . .]περ[

πέπλον[. . .]πυϛχ[

καὶ κλε[. .]ϛαω[

κροκοεντα[

πέπλον πορφυ[ρ. . . . .]δεξω[.]

χλαιναι περϛ[

ϛτέφανοι περ[

καλ[.]οϛαμ[

φρυ[

πορφ[υρ

ταπα[

[

π[

]

]

]

]

robe

and

colored with saffron

purple robe

cloaks

crowns

beautiful

]

purple

rugs

]

]

]ις . . . εγ
]ω
]μοις
]αλίαν ἔχω
] παρθένων

]

]

]

]I have

]of girls

τεθνάκην δ' ἀδόλως θέλω·
ἄ με ψιςδομένα κατελίμπανεν

πόλλα καὶ τόδ' ἔειπέ [μοι·
ὤιμ' ὡς δεῖνα πεπ[όνθ]αμεν,
Ψάπφ', ἦ μάν ς' ἀέκοις' ἀπυλιμπάνω.

τὰν δ' ἔγω τάδ' ἀμειβόμαν·
χαίροις' ἔρχεο κἄμεθεν
μέμναις', οἶςθα γὰρ ὡς <ς>ε πεδήπομεν·

αἰ δὲ μή, ἀλλά ς' ἔγω θέλω
ὄμναιςαι [. . .(.)].[. .(.)].ραι
ὀς[   ] καὶ κάλ' ἐπάςχομεν·

πό[λλοις γὰρ ςτεφάν]οις ἴων
καὶ βρ[όδων . . .]κίων τ' ὔμοι
κα. .[   ] πὰρ ἔμοι π<ε>ρεθήκα<ο >

καὶ πό.ιλλαις ὐπα.θύμιδας
πλέκιταις ἀμφ' ἀ.πάλαι δέραι
ἀνθέων ἐ[   ] πεποημέναις.

I simply want to be dead.
Weeping she left me

with many tears and said this:
Oh how badly things have turned out for us.
Sappho, I swear, against my will I leave you.

And I answered her:
Rejoice, go and
remember me. For you know how we cherished you.

But if not, I want
to remind you

       ]and beautiful times we had.

For many crowns of violets
and roses

      ]at my side you put on

and many woven garlands
made of flowers
around your soft throat.

καὶ π.....[   ]. μύρωι
βρενθείωι.[   ]ρυ[..]ν
ἐξαλ‹ε›ίψαο καὶ ‹βασ›ιληίωι

καὶ στρώμν[αν ἐ]πὶ μολθάκαν
ἀπάλαν παρ[   ]ογων
ἐξίης πόθο[ν   ].νίδων

κωὔτε τις[οὔ]τε τι
ἶρον οὐδ᾽ ὐ[   ]
ἔπλετ᾽ ὄππ[οθεν ἄμ]μες ἀπέςκομεν,

οὐκ ἄλςος .[   ].ρος
                        ]ψοφος
                        ]...οιδιαι

186

And with sweet oil
costly
you anointed yourself

and on a soft bed
delicate
you would let loose your longing

and neither any[   ]nor any
holy place nor
was there from which we were absent

no grove[   ]no dance
                   ]no sound
                   [

.ου[

ἦρ᾽ ἀ[
δηρατ.[
Γογγυλα.[

ἦ τι ϲᾶμ᾽ ἐθε.[
παιϲι μάλιϲτα.[
μαϲ γ᾽ ε̣ἰϲηλθ᾽ ἐπ.[

εἶπον· ὦ δέϲποτ᾽, ἐπ.[
ο]ὐ μὰ γὰρ μάκαιραν [
ο]ὐδὲν ἄδομ᾽ ἔπαρθ᾽ ἀγα[

κατθάνην δ᾽ ἴμερός τις [ἔχει με καὶ
λωτίνοις δροϲόεντας [ὄ-
χ[θ]οις ἴδην Ἀχερ[

.]..δεϲαιδ.[
.].γδετογ[
μητιϲε̣[

95

not

]
]
Gongyla

surely a sign
for children mostly
came in [

I said, O master
I swear no
I take no pleasure

but a kind of yearning has hold of me—to die
and to look upon the dewy lotus banks
of Acheron

]
]
]

]ϲαρδ.[. .]
πόλ]λακι τυίδε̄ [.]ων ἔχοιϲα

ὠϲπ.[. . .].ώομεν, .[. . .]..χ[. .]
 ϲε θεαϲικελαν ἀρι-
  γνωτα, ϲᾶι δὲ μάλιϲτ᾽ ἔχαιρε μόλπαι·

νῦν δὲ Λύδαιϲιν ἐμπρέπεται γυναί-
 κεϲϲιν ὥϲ ποτ᾽ ἀελίω
  δύντος ἀ βροδοδάκτυλος ‹ϲελάννα›

πάντα περ‹ρ›έχοιϲ᾽ ἄϲτρα· φάος δ᾽ ἐπί-
 ϲχει θάλαϲϲαν ἐπ᾽ ἀλμύραν
  ἴϲως καὶ πολυανθέμοις ἀρούραις·

ἀ δ᾽ ‹ἐ›έρϲα κάλα κέχυται, τεθά-
 λαιϲι δὲ βρόδα κἄπαλ᾽ ἄν-
  θρυϲκα καὶ μελίλωτος ἀνθεμώδης·

πόλλα δὲ ζαφοίταις᾽ ἀγάνας ἐπι-
 μνάϲθειϲ᾽ Ἄτθιδος ἱμέρωι
  λέπταν ποι φρένα κ[.]ρ... βόρηται·

]Sardis

often turning her thoughts here

]

you like a goddess

and in your song most of all she rejoiced.

But now she is conspicuous among Lydian women

as sometimes at sunset

the rosyfingered moon

surpasses all the stars. And her light

stretches over salt sea

equally and flowerdeep fields.

And the beautiful dew is poured out

and roses bloom and frail

chervil and flowering sweetclover.

But she goes back and forth remembering

gentle Atthis and in longing

she bites her tender mind

κῆθι δ' ἔλθην ἄμμ.[. .] . .ιϲα τόδ' οὐ
   νωνται[. .]υϲτϙνυμ[. .(.)] πόλυς
      γαρύει [. .(.)]αλον[. . . . .(.)]τϙ μέϲϲον·

ε]ΰμαρ[εϲ μ]ὲν οὐ.α.μι θέαιϲι μόρ-
   φαν ἐπή[ρατ]ον ἐξίϲω-
      ϲθαι ϲυ[. .]ϙϙϲ ἔχη‹ι›ϲθα[. . .].νίδηον

[   ]τϙ[. . .(.)]ϙατι-
   μαλ[   ].εϙοϲ
      καὶ δ[.]μ[   ]οϲ Ἀφροδίτα

καμ[   ] νέκταϙ ἔχευ' ἀπὺ
   χρυϲίαϲ [   ]γαν
      . . .(.)]απουϙ[   ] χέϙϲι Πείθω

[   ]θ[. .]ηϲενη
   [   ]ακιϲ
   [   ]. . . . . .αι

[   ]εϲ τὸ Γεραίϲτιον
   [   ]γ φίλαι
   [   ]υϲτον οὐδενο[

[   ]εϙον ἰξο[μ

But to go there
　　　　]much
　　　　　　　talks[

Not easy for us
　　　　to equal goddesses in lovely form
]

]

　　　　　　　]desire
　　　　　　　　　　and[　　　]Aphrodite

]nectar poured from
　　　　gold
　　　　　　]with hands Persuasion

]

　　　]

　　　　　]

]into the Geraistion
　　　　]beloveds
　　　　　　]of none

]into desire I shall come

. .]. θος· ἀ γὰρ μ᾽ἐγένναɩτ

ς]φᾶς ἐπ᾽ ἀλικίας μέγɩαν
κ]όςμον αἴ τις ἔχη φόβα‹ɩ›ς[
πορφύρωι κατελιξαμέɩνα

ἔμμεναι μάλα τοῦτο. [
ἀλλα ξανθοτέρα‹ɩ›ς ἔχηɩ[
τα‹ɩ›ς κόμα‹ɩ›ς δάϊδος προφ[

ς]τεφάνοιϲιν ἐπαρτίαɩɩς
ἀνθέων ἐριθαλέων· [
μ]ɩτράναν δ᾽ ἀρτίως κλ[

ποικίλαν ἀπὺ Cαρδίωɩν
. . .]. αονίας πόλ‹ε›ις [

]for my mother

in her youth it was a great
ornament if someone had hair
bound with purple—

a very great ornament indeed
But for the one who has hair yellower
than a pinetorch

crowns
of blooming flowers
and just lately a headbinder

spangled from Sardis
        ]cities

ςοὶ δ' ἔγω Κλέι ποικίλαν [
οὐκ ἔχω — πόθεν ἔςςεται; — [
μιτράν‹αν›· ἀλλὰ τὼι Μυτιληνάωι [

].[
παι.α.ειον ἔχην πο.[
αἰκε.η ποικιλαςκ...(.) [

ταῦτα τὰς Κλεανακτιδα[
φύγας..ιςαπολιςεχει
μνάματ'·.ἴδε γὰρ αἶνα διέρρυε[ν

but for you Kleis I have no
spangled—where would I get it?—
headbinder: yet the Mytilinean[

                    ] [
                    ]to hold
                    ]spangled

these things of the Kleanaktidai
exile
memories   terribly leaked away

ἀμφὶ δ' ἄβροις᾽ < > λαϲίοιϲ᾽ εὖ ⟨F⟩ ἐπύκαϲϲεν

and with delicate woven cloths covered her up well

χερρόμακτρα δὲ καγγόνων
πορφύραι καταυταμενὰ-
τατιμάϛεις ἔπεμψ' ἀπὺ Φωκάας
δῶρα τίμια καγγόνων

handcloths

purple

she sent from Phokaia

valuable gifts

Γλύκηα μᾶτερ, οὔ τοι δύναμαι κρέκην τὸν ἴϲτον
πόθωι δάμειϲα παῖδοϲ βραδίναν δι' Ἀφροδίταν

sweet mother I cannot work the loom

I am broken with longing for a boy by slender Aphrodite

].εν τὸ γὰρ ἔννεπε[.]η πϱοβ[

].ατε τὰν εὔποδα νύμφαν [

]τα παῖδα Κϱονίδα τὰν ἰόκ[ολπ]ον [

].ς ὄϱγαν θεμένα τὰν ἰόκ[ολ]πος α[

].. ἄγναι Χάϱιτες Πιέϱιδέ[ς τε] Μοῖ[ϲαι

].[. ὄ]ππότ ἀοιδαι φϱέν[...]αν.[

]ϲαιοιϲα λιγύϱαν [ἀοί]δαν

γά]μβϱον, ἄϲαϱοι γὰϱ ὑμαλικ[

]ϲε φόβαιϲι‹ν› θεμένα λύϱα.[

].. η χϱυϲοπέδιλ[ο]ϲ Αὔως [

]yes tell

]the bride with beautiful feet

]child of Kronos with violets in her lap

]setting aside anger the one with violets in her lap

]pure Graces and Pierian Muses

]whenever songs, the mind

]listening to a clear song

]bridegroom

]her hair placing the lyre

]Dawn with gold sandals

]⟩⟩⟩⟩⟩⟩⟩⟩⟩⟩ ϲμικρ[
]θην   τὰν ϲφ[
]οιϲ   πολλα[
 ]   πρὶγ γα[

 ]οι   πόλλαιϲ[
]   τὼν ϲφῶ[ν
]   ὠδαμελ[
]   χει[
]

     Γόργ

εἰς Κυπ[
ι — —.[
— — — τ[
— — — ωγ[
—

]small
]
]many
]

]many
]their
]
]
]
]Gorgo

to Kypris
]
]
]
]

]ϱηον θαλάμω τωδες[
  ]ις εὔποδα νύμφαν ἀβ[
      ] νυνδ[
     ]ν μοι·[
      ]ας γε [

103B

]of the chamber
]bride with beautiful feet
]now
]for me
]

]προλ[
]φερην[
] ιδεθελ[
Ἀρ]χεάνασσα[
]δήποτ᾽ ὀνα[
]νασαμέν[
]εν ἐπηρατ[
]ν[

]α.[
ἔ]κλυον ε[
]ρανγ..δες δ[
πα]ρθενικαις.[
].μ[
].[

]
]to carry
]
]Archeanassa
]once
]
]in lovely
]

]
]they heard
]
]maidens
]
]

104A

῎Εςπερε πάντα φέρηις ὄςα φαίνολις ἐςκέδας᾽ Αὔως,
φέρηις ὄιν, φέρηις αἶγα, φέρηις ἄπυ μάτερι παῖδα.

104B

ἀςτέρων πάντων ὀ κάλλιςτος

104A

Evening
          you gather back
               all that dazzling dawn has put asunder:
                                   you gather a lamb
                    gather a kid
gather a child to its mother

104B

of all stars the most beautiful

οἶον τὸ γλυκύμαλον ἐρεύθεται ἄκρωι ἐπ' ὔςδωι,
ἄκρον ἐπ' ἀκροτάτωι, λελάθοντο δὲ μαλοδρόπηες·
οὐ μὰν ἐκλελάθοντ', ἀλλ' οὐκ ἐδύναντ' ἐπίκεςθαι

οἴαν τὰν ὑάκινθον ἐν ὤρεςι ποίμενες ἄνδρες
πόςςι καταςτείβοιςι, χάμαι δέ τε πόρφυρον ἄνθος

105A

as the sweetapple reddens on a high branch
    high on the highest branch and the applepickers forgot—
no, not forgot: were unable to reach

105B

like the hyacinth in the mountains that shepherd men
with their feet trample down and on the ground the purple
    flower

πέρροχος, ὡς ὅτ᾽ ἄοιδος ὁ Λέσβιος ἀλλοδάποισιν

outstanding as the Lesbian singer compared to those
elsewhere

ἦρ' ἔτι παρθενίας ἐπιβάλλομαι;

do I still yearn for my virginity?

ὦ κάλα, ὦ χαρίεςςα κόρα

O beautiful O graceful one

δώςομεν, ᾗςι πάτηρ

we shall give, says father

Θυρώρωι πόδες ἑπτορόγυιοι,
τὰ δὲ ϲάμβαλα πεμπεβόεια,
πίϲϲυγγοι δὲ δέκ᾽ ἐξεπόνηϲαν

the doorkeeper's feet are seven armlengths long

                               five oxhides for his sandals

                    ten shoemakers worked on them

Ἴψοι δὴ τὸ μέλαθρον,

ὐμήναον·

ἀέρρετε, τέκτονες ἄνδρες·

ὐμήναον.

γάμβρος (εἰς)έρχεται ἶςος Ἄρευι,

⟨ὐμήναον,⟩

ἄνδρος μεγάλω πόλυ μέςδων.

⟨ὐμήναον.⟩

up with the roof!

     Hymenaios—

    lift it, carpenters!

        Hymenaios—

the bridegroom is coming in

    equal to Ares,

    Hymenaios—

       much bigger than a big man!

      Hymenaios!

Ὄλβιε γάμβρε, ϲοὶ μὲν δὴ γάμος ὡς ἄραο
ἐκτετέλεϲτ', ἔχηιϲ δὲ πάρθενον, ἂν ἄραο.
ϲοὶ χάριεν μὲν εἶδος, ὄππατα ⟨δ' ....⟩
μέλλιχ', ἔροϲ δ' ἐπ' ἰμέρτωι κέχυται προϲώπωι
⟨.............⟩ τετίμακ' ἔξοχά ϲ' Ἀφροδίτα

blest bridegroom, your marriage just as you prayed
has been accomplished

and you have the bride for whom you prayed
gracious your form and your eyes
as honey: desire is poured upon your lovely face

Aphrodite has honored you exceedingly

οὐ γὰρ
ἀτέρα νῦν πάις, ὦ γάμβρε, τεαύτα

for no
other girl
O bridegroom
such as this one now

παρθενία, παρθενία, ποῖ με λίποις' ἀ‹π›οίχηι;
οὐκέτι ἥξω πρὸς ϲέ, οὐκέτι ἥξω

virginity

    virginity

        where are you gone leaving me behind?

            no longer will I come to you

              no longer will I come

Τίωι σ', ὦ φίλε γάμβρε, κάλως ἐικάσδω;
ὄρπακι βραδίνωι σε μάλιστ' ἐικάσδω

to what

      O beloved bridegroom

            may I compare you?

                  to a slender sapling

            most of all

        do I compare you

χαῖρε, νύμφα, χαῖρε, τίμιε γάμβρε, πόλλα

farewell

    bride

        farewell

            much-honored bridegroom

117

χαίροις ἀ νύμφα, χαιρέτω δ' ὁ γάμβρος

117Α

ξοάνων προθύρων

117Β

῎Εςπερ' ὑμήναον
ὦ τὸν Ἀδώνιον

117

may you fare well
            bride
                    and let the bridegroom fare well

117A

of polished doors

117B

evening, sing Hymenaios
O the song of Adonis

ἄγι δὴ χέλυ δῖα μοι λέγε
φωνάεσςα δὲ γίνεω

yes! radiant lyre speak to me

become a voice

αἱμιτύβιον ϲτάλαϲϲον

cloth dripping

ἀλλά τις οὐκ ἔμμι παλιγκότων
ὄργαν, ἀλλ᾽ ἀβάκην τὰν φρέν᾽ ἔχω

but I am not someone who likes to wound
rather I have a quiet mind

ἀλλ' ἔων φίλος ἄμμιν λέχος ἄρνυσο νεώτερον·
οὐ γὰρ τλάσομ' ἔγω ϲύν <τ> οἴκην ἔϲϲα γεραιτέρα

but if you love us

      choose a younger bed

      for I cannot bear

            to live with you when I am the older one

ἄνθε' ἀμέργοιϲαν παῖδ' ἄγαν ἀπάλαν

gathering flowers so very delicate a girl

ἀρτίως μὲν ἀ χρυσοπέδιλος Αὔως

just now goldsandaled Dawn

αὔτα δὲ ϲὺ Καλλιόπα

and you yourself Kalliope

αυταόρα ἐϲτεφαναπλόκην

I used to weave crowns

δαύοις(') ἀπάλας ἐτα‹ί›ρας ἐν ϲτήθεϲιν

may you sleep on the breast of your delicate friend

Δεῦρο δηὖτε Μοῖϲαι χρύϲιον λίποιϲαι

127

here (once again)

Muses

leaving the gold

Δεῦτέ νυν ἅβραι Χάριτες καλλίκομοί τε Μοῖσαι

here now

      tender Graces

            and Muses with beautiful hair

ἔμεθεν δ' ἔχηιϛθα λάθαν

ἤ τιν' ἄλλον ἀνθρώπων ἔμεθεν φίληϛθα

129A

but me you have forgotten

129B

or you love some man more than me

"Ερος δηῦτέ μ' ὁ λυςιμέλης δόνει,
γλυκύπικρον ἀμάχανον ὄρπετον

Eros the melter of limbs (now again) stirs me—
sweetbitter unmanageable creature who steals in

Ἄτθι, ϲοὶ δ᾽ ἔμεθεν μὲν ἀπήχθετο
φροντίϲδην, ἐπὶ δ᾽ Ἀνδρομέδαν πότη⟨ι⟩

Atthis, to you it has become hateful

to think of me and you fly to Andromeda

Ἔςτι μοι κάλα πάις χρυςίοιςιν ἀνθέμοιςιν
ἐμφέρη‹ν› ἔχοιςα μόρφαν Κλέις ‹ › ἀγαπάτα,
ἀντὶ τᾶς ἔγωὐδὲ Λυδίαν παῖςαν οὐδ' ἐράνναν

I have a beautiful child who is like golden flowers

in form, darling Kleis

in exchange for whom I would not

all Lydia or lovely

Ἔχει μὲν Ἀνδρομέδα κάλαν ἀμοίβαν

Ψάπφοι, τί τὰν πολύολβον Ἀφροδίταν....;

Andromeda has a fine exchange

Sappho, why?

Aphrodite giver of blessings

Zὰ <.> ἐλεξάμαν ὄναϱ Κυπϱογενηα

I conversed with you in a dream

                    Kyprogeneia

Τί με Πανδίονις, ὦ Εἴρανα, χελίδων....;

why does Pandion's daughter

O Eirana

the swallow

ἦρος ἄγγελος ἱμερόφωνος ἀήδων

messenger of spring

      nightingale with a voice of longing

θέλω τί τ' εἴπην, ἀλλά με κωλύει
αἴδως ...

. . . .

[αἰ δ' ἦχες ἔςλων ἴμερον ἢ κάλων
καὶ μή τί τ' εἴπην γλῶςς' ἐκύκα κάκον,
αἴδως κέν ςε οὐκ ἦχεν ὄππατ',
    ἀλλ' ἔλεγες περὶ τῶ δικαίω]

I want to say something but shame
prevents me

yet if you had a desire for good or beautiful things
and your tongue were not concocting some evil to say,
shame would not hold down your eyes
but rather you would speak about what is just

ϲτᾶθι κἄντα φίλοϲ
καὶ τὰν ἐπ᾽ ὄϲϲοιϲ᾽ ὀμπέταϲον χάριν

stand to face me beloved

and open out the grace of your eyes

Κατθνάςκει, Κυθέρη', ἄβρος Ἄδωνις· τί κε θεῖμεν;
καττύπτεςθε, κόραι, καὶ κατερείκεςθε χίτωνας

delicate Adonis is dying

        Kythereia

            what should we do?

                  strike yourselves

           maidens

  and tear your garments

κῆ δ' ἀμβροςίας μὲν
κράτηρ ἐκέκρατ'
   Ἔρμαις δ' ἔλων ὄλπιν θέοις' ἐοινοχόηςε.
κῆνοι δ' ἄρα πάντες
καρχάςι' ἦχον
   κἄλειβον· ἀράςαντο δὲ πάμπαν ἔςλα γάμβρωι

but there a bowl of ambrosia

    had been mixed

        and Hermes taking the jug poured wine for

      the gods

and then they all

    held cups

        and poured libation and prayed every

        good thing for the bridegroom

Λάτω καὶ Νιόβα μάλα μὲν φίλαι ἦσαν ἕταιραι

Leto and Niobe were beloved friends

χρύϲειοι ⟨δ'⟩ ἐρέβινθοι ἐπ' ἀϊόνων ἐφύοντο

and gold chickpeas were growing on the banks

μάλα δὴ κεκορημένοις

Γόργως

to those who have quite had their fill

of Gorgo

μὴ κίνη χέραδος

145

do not move stones

μήτε μοι μέλι μήτε μέλιϲϲα

neither for me honey nor the honey bee

μνάϲεϲθαί τινα φα‹ῖ›μι καὶ ἕτερον ἀμμέων

someone will remember us

        I say

            even in another time

ὁ πλοῦτος ἄνευ ἀρέτας οὐκ ἀσίνης πάροικος
ἁ δ' ἀμφοτέρων κρᾶσις εὐδαιμονίας ἔχει τὸ ἄκρον

wealth without virtue is no harmless neighbor

but a mixture of both attains the height of happiness

ὄτα πάννυχος ἄϲφι κατάγρει

when all night long

       it pulls them down

οὐ γὰρ θέμις ἐν μοισοπόλων ⟨δόμωι⟩

θρῆνον ἔμμεν᾿ ⟨. . . . . . .⟩ οὔ κ᾿ ἄμμι πρέποι τάδε

for it is not right in a house of the Muses

that there be lament

this would not become us

ὀφθάλμοις δὲ μέλαις νύκτος ἄωρος

and on the eyes

        black sleep of night

παντοδάπαις‹ι› μεμ‹ε›ιχμένα χροίαισιν

mingled with all kinds of colors

πάρθενον ἀδύφωνον

girl sweetvoiced

Πλήρης μὲν ἐφαίνετ' ἀ ϲελάν‹ν›α,
αἰ δ' ὡϲ περὶ βῶμον ἐϲτάθηϲαν

full appeared the moon
and when they around the altar took their places

πόλλα μοι τὰν Πωλυανάκτιδα παῖδα χαίρην

a very long farewell to the child of Polyanaktides

πόλυ πάκτιδος ἀδυμελεϲτέρα

χρύϲω χρυϲοτέρα

far more sweetsounding than a lyre
golder than gold

πότνια Αὔως

lady Dawn

ςκιδναμένας ἐν ςτήθεςιν ὄργας

μαψυλάκαν γλῶςςαν πεφύλαχθαι

with anger spreading in the chest
to guard against a vainly barking tongue

ςύ τε κᾶμος θεράπων Ἔρος

both you and my servant Eros

τάδε νῦν ἐταίραις
ταὶς ἔμαις τέρπνα κάλως ἀείσω

these things now for my companions

                I shall sing beautifully

τανδεφυλάςςετε ἐννε[. .]οι γάμβροι [. . . . .]υ πολίων βαςίληες

guard her
bridegrooms
kings of cities

τίοισιν ὀφθάλμοισι(ν);

with what eyes?

τὸ μέλημα τὦμον

my darling one

τὸν Ϝὸν παῖδα κάλει

she summons her son

φαίνεταί Ϝοι κῆνος

that man seems to himself

φαῖα δή ποτα Λήδαν ὐακίνθινον
< . . . > ὤϊον εὔρην πεπυκάδμενον

they say Leda once found a hyacinth-colored

egg hidden

ὠίω πόλυ λευκότερον

whiter by far than an egg

ὦ τὸν Ἄδωνιν

O for Adonis

Γέλλως παιδοφιλωτέρα

who loves children more than Gello

Δέδυκε μὲν ἀ ϲελάννα
καὶ Πληΐαδεϲ· μέϲαι δὲ
νύκτεϲ, παρὰ δ' ἔρχετ' ὦρα,
ἔγω δὲ μόνα κατεύδω.

Moon has set
and Pleiades: middle
night, the hour goes by,
alone I lie.

ποικίλλεται μὲν
γαῖα πολυστέφανος

168C

spangled is
the earth with her crowns

169

ἀγαγοίην

169A

ἀθρήματα

170

Αἶγα

171

ἄκακος

172

ἀλγεσίδωρος

169

I would lead

169A

wedding gifts

170

Aiga

171

non-evil

172

paingiver

173

ἀμαμάξυδ(-ος, -ες)

174

[ἀμάρα]

175

αὖα

176

βάρβιτος. βάρωμος. βάρμος.

177

βεῦδος

173

a vine that grows up trees

174

channel

175

dawn

176

lyre lyre lyre

177

transparent dress

179

γρύτα

180

Ἕκτωρ

181

ζάβατον

182

ἰοίην

183

κατώρης / κατάρης

179

makeup bag

180

holder

181

crossable

182

I might go

183

downrushing

184

κίνδυν

185

μελίφωνος

186

μήδεϊα

187

Μοισάων

188

μυθόπλοκος

184

danger

185

honeyvoiced

186

Medeia

187

of the Muses

188

mythweaver

189

νίτρον

190

πολυΐδριδι

191

ϲέλιν‹ν›α

192

χρυϲαϲτράγαλοι φίαλαι

189

soda

190

manyskilled

191

celery

192

gold anklebone cups

NOTES

1.1 "of the spangled mind": two different readings of the first word of Sappho's first fragment have descended to us from antiquity: *poikilothron'* (printed by Lobel, Page, Campbell and Voigt) and *poikilophron* (printed here). The word is a compound adjective, used as an epithet of Aphrodite to identify either her "chair" *(thron-)* or her "mind" *(phron-)* as *poikilos*: "many-colored, spotted, dappled, variegated, intricate, embroidered, inlaid, highly wrought, complicated, changeful, diverse, abstruse, ambiguous, subtle." Now certainly the annals of ancient furniture include some fancy chairs, especially when gods sit on them; and initial mention of her throne provides an elegant point of departure for the downrush of Aphrodite's next motion. On the other hand, it is Aphrodite's agile mind that seems to be at play in the rest of the poem and, since compounds of *thron-* are common enough in Greek poetry to make this word predictable, perhaps Sappho relied on our ear to supply the chair while she went on to spangle the mind.

Other examples of the adjective *poikilos* or its compounds occur in Sappho frr. 39.2, 44.9, 98a11, 98b1, 98b6; cf. also Alkaios fr. 345.2 (of a bird's throat) and fr. 69.7 (of a man with a mind like a fox).

1.15, 16, 18 "(now again)": the parentheses are not Sappho's but I want to mark her use of the temporal adverb *dēute*. It is probably no accident that, in a poem about the cyclical patterns of erotic experience, this adverb of repetition is given three times. (Also repeated are the adjective that characterizes Aphrodite's relation to time—"deathless," occurring twice; Aphrodite's questions to Sappho, refracted four ways; and Aphrodite's final erotic rule, given three formulations.) The adverb is a compound of two words, *dē* and *aute,* contracted for euphonic reasons into *dēute*. *Dē* is a particle signifying vividly that some event is taking place in the present moment; it strikes a note of powerful alert emotion (sometimes with a tinge of irony or skepticism), like English "Well now!" *Aute* is an adverb that peers past the present moment to a series of repeated actions stretching behind; it intercepts the new and binds it into history, as if to say "Not for the first time!" Sappho's "(now again)" does more than mark repetition as a theme of her poem, it instantiates the difference between mortal and immortal perspectives on this painful feature of erotic life: Sappho is stuck in the pain of the "now," Aphrodite calmly surveys a larger pattern of "agains."

For other instances of the adverb *dēute* in Sappho see frr. 22.11; 83.4; 127; 130.1.

1.18–24 Sappho's reverie goes transparent at the center when she shifts midverse to direct speech of Aphrodite. There is an eerie casualness to the immortal voice simply present within Sappho's own, which some translators modify with quotation marks or italics. This poem is cast in the form of a hymn or prayer, how straightforwardly is hard to say. Hymnic features include the opening catalogue of divine epithets, central reverie concerned with former epiphanies of the god, repetition of a plea at the beginning and the end ("come here . . . come to me"). For other literary examples of prayers see Homer *Iliad* 5.116ff; 10.284ff; 16.233ff; Pindar *Isthmians* 6.42ff; Sophokles *Oedipus the King* 163ff; Aristophanes *Thesmophoriazousai* 1156ff.

2.1 "here": adverb of place that means "hither, to this place" with verbs of motion or "here, in this place" with verbs of rest, often used as an interjection "Come on! Here now!" when followed by an imperative verb. Notice that the imperative verb evoked by this adverb, for which the whole poem with its slow weight of onomatopoeically accumulating clauses seems to be waiting, does not arrive until the very last word: "pour" (16). Arrival is the issue, for it sanctifies waiting: *attente de Dieu*. The poem is a hymn of the type called "kletic," that is, a calling hymn, an invocation to god to come from where she is to where we are. Such a hymn typically names both of these places, setting its invocation in between so as to measure the difference—a difference exploded as soon as the hymn achieves its aim. Inherent in the rationale of a kletic hymn, then, is an emptiness or distance that it is the function of the hymn to mark by an act of attention. Sappho suspends attention between adverb at the beginning and verb at the end: the effect is uncanny—as if creation could be seen waiting for an event that is already perpetually *here*. There is no clear boundary between far and near; there is no climactic moment of god's arrival. Sappho renders a set of conditions that at the beginning depend on Aphrodite's absence but by the end include her presence—impossible drop that saturates the world. "God can only be present in creation under the form of absence," says Simone Weil, in *Gravity and Grace,* translated by Arthur Wills (Lincoln, Nebraska, 1997), 162.

2.8 "sleep": *kōma* is a noun used in the Hippokratic texts of the lethargic state called "coma" yet not originally a medical term. This is the profound, weird, sexual sleep that enwraps Zeus after love with Hera (Homer *Iliad* 14.359); this is the punishing, unbreathing stupor imposed for a year on any god who breaks an oath (Hesiod *Theogony* 798); this is the trance of attention induced by listening to music of the lyre (Pindar *Pythians* 1.12); this is the deep religious stillness described by Gregory of Nazianzus in a Christian poem from the fourth century A.D. that appears to be modeled on Sappho's, for Gregory imagines himself awaiting his god in a garden:

> Breezes whispered . . .
> lavishing beautiful sleep [*koma*] from the tops of the trees
> on my heart so very weary.
> > —*Patrologia graeca* 37, ed. J. P. Migne (Paris, 1862), 755ff.

Otherworldliness is intensified in Sappho's poem by the synaesthetic quality of her *kōma*—dropping from leaves set in motion by a shiver of light over the tree: Sappho's adjective *aithussomenon* ("radiant-shaking," 7) blends visual and tactile perceptions with a sound of rushing emptiness.

2.14 "gold cups": not mortal tableware, nor is nectar a beverage normally enjoyed by any but gods (along with ambrosia, e.g., *Odyssey* 5.92–4).

3.11 "all night long": if this reading (Diehl's 1923 conjecture) is correct, Sappho may be pursuing her own night thoughts (Diehl thinks these thoughts concern her brother: cf. frr. 5, 7, 15) or else participating in a nocturnal ritual. Allnight rites *(pannuchides)* were a feature of ancient Greek worship and turn up in literature, for example, Euripides describes a chorus invoking Athena:

> On the windy mountain ridge
> shrill voices of girls
> echo to the beat all night
> of feet dancing.
> > —*Heraklaidai* 777–8.

See also Sappho frr. 23.13, 30.3, 149; and H. W. Parke, *Festivals of the Athenians* (London, 1977), 49.

Secular reasons for insomnia may also be part of the Sapphic tradition, according to the fourth-century A.D. orator Libanius:

> So if nothing prevented the Lesbian Sappho from praying that her night be made twice as long, let it be permitted me too to pray for something like this.
>
> —Libanius *Orations* 12.99 = Sappho fr. 197 Voigt

Libanius doesn't say why Sappho made this prayer but it brings to mind a passage of Homer's *Odyssey*, where Athene "slows down the night" for the newly reunited Odysseus and Penelope by stalling the horses of Dawn on the edge of Ocean (23.242–6; cf. also the battle of Amorites and Israelites in *Joshua* 10.13).

4.9 "having been stained": depending on how the first letter of this word is restored it may mean also "having been touched on the surface, caressed" or "having been tainted, defiled."

5.2 "brother": ancient sources name three brothers of Sappho, of whom the eldest, Charaxos, made himself notorious by his pursuit of a courtesan (Rhodopis) not mentioned in this poem but see below frr. 7 and 15.

7.1 "Doricha": ancient sources suggest this is one name of a courtesan favored by Sappho's brother Charaxos. Herodotos relates:

> Rhodopis arrived in Egypt . . . to ply her trade but was redeemed at a high price by a man from Mytilene—Charaxos, brother of the poet Sappho. . . . And when Charaxos returned to Mytilene after liberating Rhodopis Sappho rebuked him severely in a poem.
>
> (2.134ff)

Strabo adds:

> The woman whom Herodotos calls Rhodopis is named Doricha by Sappho.
>
> (17.1.33)

So too Athenaios:

> Naukratis attracted celebrity prostitutes, like Doricha, who was the beloved of Sappho's brother Charaxos and whom Sappho attacked in verse on the

grounds that she got a lot of money out of Charaxos. . . . But Herodotos calls her Rhodopis.

(13.596b–d)

And an epigrammatist of the Hellenistic period wrote this poem about her:

> Doricha, your bones fell asleep long ago
> > and your hair and the perfume-breathing cloth
> in which you once wrapped graceful Charaxos,
> > close by his flesh, when you drank the dawn.
> But the singing white pages of Sappho's love songs live on
> > and will live on.
> Blessed is your name which Naukratis is to guard
> > so long as a Nile boat sails the salt sea.
> > > —Posidippos xvii *The Greek Anthology* Gow-Page

Rhodopis ("face like a rose") could be a professional name that Sappho scruples to use.

8.3 "Atthis": Sappho's relationship with Atthis was controversial, according to the ancient lexicographer:

> Sappho had three companions and friends, Atthis, Telesippa, Megara. Through her relations with them she got a reputation for shameful love.
> > —*Suda* s.v. Sappho

Maximus of Tyre reads the matter philosophically:

> The *eros* of the Lesbian woman—what else could it be than the Sokratic art of love? For they seem to me to have practiced love each after their own fashion, she the love of women and he the love of men. They both said they loved many and were captured by all things beautiful. What Alkibiades and Charmides and Phaidros were to Sokrates, Gyrinna and Atthis and Anaktoria were to the Lesbian woman. And what the rival artists Prodykos and Gorgias and Thrasymachos and Protagoras were to Sokrates, Gorgo and Andromeda were to Sappho. Sometimes she rebukes them, sometimes she interrogates them and she makes use of irony just like Sokrates.
> > —*Orations* 18.9

See also Sappho frr. 49, 96, 131.

16.1–4 "some men say . . . some men say . . . some men say . . . but I say":
Sappho begins with a rhetorical device called a priamel, whose function is to focus attention and to praise. The priamel's typical structure is a list of three items followed by a fourth that is different and better. Sappho's list marshals three stately masculine opinions, then curves into dissent. Her dissent will solidify as Helen in the next stanza.

On the priamel see B. Snell, *The Discovery of the Mind,* translated by T. G. Rosenmeyer (Cambridge, Mass., 1953), 47–50; A. P. Burnett, *Three Archaic Poets: Archilochus, Alcaeus, Sappho* (Cambridge, Mass., 1983), 281–5; W. H. Race, *The Classical Priamel from Homer to Boethius* (Leiden, 1982); J. J. Winkler, *The Constraints of Desire* (New York, 1990), 176–7; and cf. Bakkhylides 3.85–92; Pindar *Olympians* 1.1–7; Plato *Lysis* 211d–e; Tyrtaios 9.1–14 West.

16.12–16 Because of the corruption of these central verses it is impossible to say who led Helen astray (could be Aphrodite, Eros, or some principle of delusion like Atē) or how Sappho managed the transition from Helen to Anaktoria "who is gone." It is a restless and strangely baited poem that seems to gather its logic into itself rather than pay it out. Rather like Helen. Beauty comes out of unexpectedness, and stares at us, "as though we were the ones who'd made a mistake," as Yannis Ritsos says in a poem "Expected and Unexpected" in *Ritsos in Parentheses,* translated by E. Keeley (Princeton, 1979), 160–1.

17.2 Hera, sister and wife of Zeus, was worshipped on Lesbos at a sanctuary in or near Mytilene. The poet Alkaios, Sappho's contemporary and fellow-Lesbian, also mentions this shrine and its trinitarian worship of Zeus, Hera and Dionysos (=Thyone's child): see Alkaios fr. 129. According to a Homeric scholiast (on *Iliad* 9.129) the shrine of Hera was the site of an annual beauty contest for Lesbian women, to which Alkaios refers in fr. 130. There is also an anonymous epigram in the *Palatine Anthology* that praises this site:

> Come to the radiant precinct of bullfaced Hera,
> > Lesbian women, make your delicate feet turn.
> There set up beautiful dancing and your leader will be
> > Sappho with a gold lyre in her hands.
> Lucky ones in the glad dance: surely you will think
> > you hear Kalliope's own sweet singing.
>
> —*Palatine Anthology* 9.189

18.1 "Pan": capitalized, the first word of this fragment is Pan the god of goats, wild space, pipes and the silence of noon. Uncapitalized it is *pan,* which can be a noun ("everything") or an adjective ("every, all") or an adverb ("altogether, wholly"). Capitalization is an editorial decision: codices before the ninth century were generally written entirely in majuscule script.

21.6 "old age": Sappho treats this theme also in fr. 58 below. Commentators differ on whether to understand the speaker's chagrin as erotic, or as a professional worry on the part of a chorus leader no longer able to whirl about with the choirs of girls (as Alkman complains in his fr. 26), or as a mythic *topos* elaborated for its own sake.

21.13 "with violets in her lap": I do not know what this adjective means exactly. It is composed of the word *ion,* "violet" (which can also mean "purple" or "dark" or "like violets") and the word *kolpos,* "bosom, lap, womb; fold formed by a loose garment; any hollow." In Sappho it is an epithet of brides and of a goddess: see frr. 30.5, 103.3 and 103.4.

22.10 The name Gongyla is missing its first two letters at the beginning of this verse but appears in full in fr. 95.4 and also shows up in a second-century-A.D. papyrus commentary on Sappho that identifies Gongyla as "yoke-mate" *(synzyx)* of a woman named Gorgo (see fr. 213, 213a and 214a Voigt). No one knows what a yoke-mate is precisely. Yoking is a common figure for marriage; there is a cognate verb *(syndyazein)* that means "to unite in wedlock" and a cognate noun that means "wife" when used of females but simply "comrade" when applied to males. There is also an abstract noun *(syzygia)* used by Euripides of a collaboration between Muses and Graces in choral song *(Herakles Mad 673).* Gongyla of Kolophon is named by the *Suda* as a pupil of Sappho along with Anagora of Miletos and Eunika of Salamis.

22.11 "(now again)": See above fr. 1 and below fr. 130.

31.9 "tongue breaks": the transmitted text contains a hiatus (conjunction of two open vowels) between "tongue" *(glōssa)* and "breaks" *(eage)* that contravenes the rules of Greek metrics and convinces most editors to mark the verse as corrupt. On the other hand, the hiatus creates a ragged sound that may be meant to suggest breakdown.

For various ways of reading Sappho's broken tongue, see G. Nagy, *Comparative Studies in Greek and Indic Meter* (Cambridge, Mass., 1974), 45; D. O'Higgins, "Sappho's Splintered Tongue," *American Journal of Philology* 111 (1990), 156–67; Y. Prins, *Victorian Sappho* (Princeton, 1999), 28–73; J. Svenbro, *Phrasikleia*, translated by J. Lloyd (Ithaca, 1993), 152.

31.17 The poem has been preserved for us by the ancient literary critic Longinus (*On the Sublime* 10.1–3), who quotes four complete Sapphic stanzas, then the first verse of what looks like a fifth stanza, then breaks off, no one knows why. Sappho's account of the symptoms of desire attains a unity of music and sense in vv. 1–16, framed by verbs of seeming ("he seems to me," "I seem to me"), so if the seventeenth verse is authentic it must represent an entirely new thought. It is worth noting that Catullus' translation of the poem into Latin includes, at just this point, an entirely new thought.

Longinus' admiration for Sappho's poem is keen. He finds in it an example of a certain mode of sublimity, which is able to select the most extreme sensations of an event and combine these together "as if into one body," as he says (*On the Sublime* 10.1). He elaborates:

> Are you not amazed at how she researches all at once the soul the body the ears the tongue the eyes the skin all as if they had departed from her and belong to someone else? And contradictorily in one instant she chills, she burns, is crazy and sensible, for she is in terror or almost dead. So that no single passion is apparent in her but a confluence of passions. And her selection (as I said) of the most important elements and her combination of these into a whole achieves excellence.
>
> —*On the Sublime* 10.3

Sappho's body falls apart, Longinus' body comes together: drastic contract of the sublime.

34.5 "silvery": the adjective is not part of the text of this poem as quoted (vv. 1–4) by the grammarian Eustathios in his commentary on *Iliad* 8.555, but has been added because the Roman emperor Julian refers to the poem in a letter to the sophist Hekebolios:

Sappho . . . says the moon is silver and so hides the other stars from view.

—Julian *Epistles* 387a

On Julian cf. frr. 48, 163 and note to fr. 140 below.

37 These two bits of text are cited as Sappho's by the *Etymologicum Genuinum* in a discussion of words for pain: "And the Aeolic writers call pain a dripping . . . because it drips and flows." For "dripping" Sappho has the noun *stalygmon*, cognate with the verb *stazei* ("drips") used by Aeschylus in a passage of *Agamemnon* where the chorus is describing its own nocturnal anxiety:

> And it drips in sleep before my heart
> the grief-remembering pain.

(179–80)

We might compare this physiology of pain with the sensations noted by Hamm in Beckett's *Endgame:*

> There's something dripping in my head.
> (Pause.)
> A heart in my head.
>
> There's something dripping in my head, ever since the fontanelles.
> (Stifled hilarity of Nagg.)
> Splash, splash, always on the same spot.

—Samuel Beckett, *Endgame* (New York, 1958), 18 and 50.

38 Translation of this fragment raises the problem of pronouns in Sappho. Her Greek text actually says "us" not "me." Slippage between singular and plural in pronouns of the first person is not uncommon in ancient poetry; the traditional explanation is that much of this poetry was choral in origin, that is, performed by a chorus of voices who collectively impersonate the voice that speaks in the poem. A glance at Sappho's fragments 5, 21, 24a, 94, 96, 147, 150, all of which employ a first-person-plural pronoun where the modern ear expects singular, will show the extent of the phenomenon. I translate "us" as "us" in all those other examples. But the fragile heat of fr. 38 seems to me to evaporate entirely without a bit of intervention.

On the other hand, I may be reading this sentence all wrong. Erotic fire has a history, not only in Sappho (see fr. 48) but also in later lyric poets (e.g., Anakreon fr. 413 *PMG* and Pindar *Pythians* 4. 219). The verb I have rendered as "burn" can also be translated "bake, roast, broil, boil" and so suggest a concrete figure for the "cooking" of passion that is to be found in Hellenistic literature, e.g., in an epigram of Meleager who pictures Eros as "cook of the soul" (*Palatine Anthology* 12.92.7–8; cf. also Theokritos *Idylls* 7.55 and Kallimachos *Epigrams* 43.5). If burning means cooking and "you" is Eros, this becomes a very different poem—a cry to the god who plays with fire from the community of souls subjected to its heat.

Further on the phenomenology of desire in Sappho see G. Lanata "Sul linguaggio amoroso di Saffo," *Quaderni urbinati di cultura classica* 2 (1966), 63–79, translated by W. Robins in E. Greene, ed., *Reading Sappho* (Berkeley, 1996), 11–25.

44 In narrating a story from the Trojan War saga Sappho chooses an episode not included in the *Iliad*—the homecoming of Hektor with his bride Andromache. She adopts a version of Homer's (dactylic) meter as well as certain epic features of diction, spelling, scansion and syntax, mingling these with real details from the Lesbos of her own time like myrrh, cassia, frankincense and castanets. Some editors have thought this song about a wedding was composed to be sung at a wedding.

See C. Calame, *Les choeurs de jeunes filles en Grèce archaïque* (Rome, 1977), 1.160–3; H. Fränkel, *Early Greek Poetry and Philosophy*, translated by M. Hadas and J. Willis (New York, 1973), 174–6; F. Lasserre, *Sappho, une autre lecture* (Padua, 1989), 26–36.

44Aa and 44Ab Originally Lobel thought these fragments from a papyrus written in the second or third century A.D. should be assigned to Alkaios; other editors detect Sappho.

46 This fragment is cited by Herodian in his treatise *On Anomalous Words* because it contains a perky word for "cushion."

47 This fragment has been reconstructed by Lobel from a paraphrase in Maximus of Tyre, who compares Sappho to Sokrates as an eroticist (*Orations* 18.9).

48 The Roman emperor Julian cites this sentence in a letter that begins:

> You came yes you did—thanks to your letter you arrived even though you were absent.

> —*Epistles* 240 b–c

Julian's letter is addressed to Iamblichos, chief exponent of the Syrian school of neoplatonism, and is regarded as apocryphal because Iamblichos will have died when Julian was a child. More interesting is the problem of erotic temperature raised by emendations to the text of the main verb in the second line, which appears as *ephylaxas* ("you guarded, kept safe") in the codices—a reading that is unmetrical and therefore emended either to *ephlexas* ("you inflamed": Wesseling) or *epsyxas* ("you cooled": Thomas).

49 The first verse is cited by Hephaistion in his *Handbook* on meters (7.7) as an example of dactylic pentameter, the second verse by Plutarch in his treatise *On Love* (751d) as an example of a remark to a girl too young for marriage. A third citation by the grammarian Terentianus Maurus suggests the two verses go together.

50 Galen commends this sentiment in his *Exhortation to Learning* (8.16):

> So since we know the ripeness of youth is like spring flowers and brings brief pleasure, admire Sappho for saying . . .

51 Chrysippos cites this sentence in his treatise *On Negatives* (23). Bruno Snell's by now notorious discovery of *The Discovery of the Mind* in this Sapphic fragment is still worth considering for its irritant value. *The Discovery of the Mind,* translated by T. G. Rosenmeyer (Cambridge, Mass., 1953).

52 Herodian's citation of this sentence in his treatise *On Anomalous Words* ends with some letters no longer legible that may be something like "with my two arms."

53 The Graces (*Charites* in Greek, derived from *charis:* "grace") are three in number, embodiments of beauty or charm, companions of the Muses and attendants of Aphrodite.

54 Pollux cites this phrase in his *Onomastikon* (10.124) for its use of a new word for "cloak" *(chlamys)* and also reports that Sappho is talking here about Eros.

55.2–3 "the roses of Pieria": Pieria is a mountainous region in northern Greece which was believed to be the birthplace of the Muses; the works of the Muses—music, dance, poetry, learning, culture—are symbolized by their roses. Plutarch tells us this poem was addressed to a woman wealthy but *amousos* ("without the Muses," indifferent to their works). But the works of the Muses are also the substance of memory. Sappho's poem threatens the woman with an obliteration which it then enacts by not naming her.

55.3 "too": Sappho's word *kan* is a contraction of *kai + en* for metrical purpose (to save a beat of time) but its effect is also conceptual—to syncopate some woman's posthumous nonentity upon her present life without roses.

55.1–4 "Dead. . . . Having been breathed out": a participle in the aorist tense *(katthanoisa)* begins the poem and a participle in the perfect tense *(ekpepota-mena)* ends it. The aorist tense expresses past action as a point of fact; the perfect tense renders past action whose effect continues into the future; so does Sappho's poem softly exhale some woman from the point of death into an infinitely featureless eternity. Cognate with words for wings, flying, fluttering and breath, the participle *ekpepotamena,* with its spatter of plosives and final open vowel, sounds like the escape of a soul into nothingness.

56 Chrysippos cites these lines (as prose) in his treatise *On Negatives* (13). The word translated "wisdom" *(sophia)* may connote "skill" or "learning" of any kind—possibly poetic skill.

57 Amid a collection of sartorial anecdotes Athenaios cites the first and third line of this fragment, informing us that Sappho is making fun of Andromeda as Plato does of "men who do not know how to throw their cloak over their shoulder from left to right nor how to put words together in proper harmony for praising gods and men" (*Theaetetus* 175e; *Deipnosophistai* 21b–c). The second verse of the fragment comes from Maximus of Tyre (*Orations* 18.9), who compares Sappho's comment on Andromeda with Sokrates' satire of the sophists' fashion sen *(schēma)* and habit of reclining *(kataklisis)*. For Andromeda see fr. 68a and note on fr. 8 above.

58.25 "delicacy" *(abrosynē):* could also be translated "fineness," "luxuriance," "daintiness" or "refined sensuality." In the late sixth century B.C. the word came to designate a certain kind of luxurious "eastern" lifestyle cultivated by an aristocratic elite that wished to distinguish itself this way. In other poems Sappho uses the cognate adjective or adverb to describe Adonis (fr. 140), the Graces (fr. 128), Andromache (fr. 44.7), linen (fr. 100), a woman (25.4), the action of pouring nectar (2.14). See L. Kurke, "The Politics of ἁβροσύνη in Archaic Greece," *Classical Antiquity* 11 (1992), 90–121.

58.25–6: These words may also be construed to mean:

> But I love delicacy [   ] this
> and desire for the sun has won me brilliance and beauty.

The question remains, What is the relevance of either "desire for the sun" or "beauty of the sun" here? It has been suggested that the poem refers to the myth of Tithonos, a young man so desirable that the goddess of Dawn (Auos or Eos) fell in love with him and rapt him away to the ends of the earth. She then asked Zeus to give him immortal life but forgot to request immortal youth, so Tithonos aged forever.

See E. Stehle, "Sappho's Gaze: Fantasies of a Goddess and a Young Man," *differences* 2 (1990), 88–125; G. Nagy, "Phaethon, Sappho's Phaon and the White Rock of Leukas," *Harvard Studies in Classical Philology* 77 (1973), 137–77.

68a.5 and 68a.12 For Andromeda and Megara see note on fr. 8 above.

81 Parts of three verses at the beginning are transmitted on papyrus; the rest is cited by Athenaios in a discussion of the use of garlands (*Deipnosophistai* 15.674e).

82a and 82b In his metrical *Handbook* of the second century A.D. Hephaistion cites the phrase "Mnasidika more finely shaped than soft Gyrinno" as an example of acatalectic tetrameter (=82a). About a thousand years later this same phrase turned up on a papyrus along with the beginnings of four other verses (=82b). For Gyrinno (if she is the same person as Gyrinna) see note on fr. 8 above.

91 Some editors think these words cited by Hephaistion in his metrical *Handbook* (11.5) are actually the first verse of fr. 60 above.

Eirana is either a woman's name or the word for "peace." If it is "peace" Sappho is presumably talking about erotic warfare (note fr. 60 contains the verb "to fight").

94.1 "to be dead" or "to have died": the poem's first word is a perfect active infinitive denoting a past action (death) that slides into the present (as death wish). Sliding from past to present, from present to past, is Sappho's method in this poem and she seems to offer it (the sliding screen of memory) as a consolation to the woman who weeps while going. Because the beginning of the poem is lost, as the metrical scheme indicates, it remains unclear whether it is Sappho or the weeping woman who wishes for death.

See G. Lanata, "Sul linguaggio amoroso di Saffo," *Quaderni urbinati di cultura classica* 2 (1966), 63–79, translated by W. Robins in E. Greene, ed., *Reading Sappho* (Berkeley, 1996), 19–20; T. McEvilley, "Sappho Fr. 94," *Phoenix* 25 (1971), 1–11; E. Robbins, "Who's Dying in Sappho Fr. 94?" *Phoenix* 44 (1990), 111–21; J. M. Snyder, *The Woman and the Lyre* (Carbondale, 1989), 26.

95.7 In between "mostly" and "came in" are traces of letters that might be reconstructed to form the name of Hermes, who traditionally guided souls to the land of the dead.

95.11–13 "yearning . . .": Sappho associates desire with death in fr. 31.15–16 and fr. 94.1 above; cf. also Anakreon's erotic complaint "may I die as I can find no other loosening from these pains" (fr. 411 PMG); Alkman's description of desire as a "more melting than sleep or death" (fr. 3.61–2 PMG); Oedipus' "longing to look upon the hearth of my father underground" (Sophokles *Oedipus at Colonus* 1725–7).

96.1 "Sardis": capital city of the rich kingdom of Lydia in Asia Minor, Sardis was commercial center and said to be the place where coinage was invented.

96.3 "you": compare this triangular reverie of moonlit women with that of Emily Dickinson's letter to Susan Gilbert, October 9, 1851:

I wept a tear here, Susie, on purpose for *you*—because this "sweet silver moon" smiles in on me and Vinnie, and then it goes so far before it gets to you—and then you never told me if there *was* any moon in Baltimore—and how do *I* know Susie—that you see her sweet face at all? She looks like a fairy tonight, sailing around the sky in a little silver gondola with stars for gondoliers. I asked her to let me ride a little while ago—and told her I would *get out* when she got as far as Baltimore, but she only smiled to herself and went sailing on.

I think she was quite ungenerous—but I have learned the lesson and shant ever ask her again. To day it rained at home—sometimes it rained so hard that I fancied you could hear it's patter—patter, patter, as it fell upon the leaves—and the fancy pleased me so, that I sat and listened to it—and watched it earnestly. *Did* you hear it Susie—or was it *only* fancy? Bye and bye the sun came out—just in time to bid us goodnight, and as I told you sometime, the moon is shining now.

It is such an evening Susie, as you and I would walk and have such pleasant musings, if you were only here—perhaps we would have a "Reverie" after the form of "Ik Marvel", indeed I do not know why it would'nt be just as charming as of that lonely Bachelor, smoking his cigar—and it would be far more profitable as "Marvel" *only* marvelled, and you and I would *try* to make a little destiny to have for our own.

—*Letters of Emily Dickinson* 1.143–4

More explicitly than Sappho, Emily Dickinson evokes the dripping fecundity of daylight as foil for the mind's voyaging at night. Almost comically, she personifies the moon as chief navigator of the liquid thoughts that women like to share in the dark, in writing. And perhaps Ik Marvel (a popular author of the day, who dwelt upon his own inner life in bestselling "Reveries") is a sort of Homeric prototype—out of whose clichés she may startle a bit of destiny for herself.

96.7 "rosyfingered": an adjective used habitually by Homer to designate the red look of Dawn. I think Sappho means to be startling, but I don't know *how* startling, when she moves the epithet to a nocturnal sky. Also startling is the fecundity of sea, field and memory which appears to flow from this uncanny moon and fill the nightworld of the poem—swung from a thread of "as sometimes" in verse 7. Homer too liked to extend a simile this way, creating a parallel surface of such tangibility it rivals the main story for a minute. Homer is more concerned than Sappho to keep the borders of the two surfaces intact; epic arguably differs from lyric precisely in the way it manages such rivalry.

98a.3 "ornament" or "good order" (*kosmos* = English "cosmos"): a word that implies all sorts of order, from the arrangement of planets in the sky at night to the style with which an individual wears her hat. In the language of politics, *kosmos* means the constitution or good government of a city. In the language of cosmology, *kosmos* means the entire, perfect, ordered universe. According to one ancient cosmology, cosmos was first assembled out of chaos, when Zeus threw a veil over the head of the goddess of the underworld, Chthoniē, and married her. So Pherekydes tells us, and he goes on to describe the veil, on which were embroidered earth, ocean and the houses of ocean—that is to say, the contours of the civilized world. Once veiled by her bridegroom, the dark and formless chthonic goddess was transformed and renamed Gē, goddess of the visible world, decorous and productive wife of Zeus (Pherekydes frr. 50–4 Diels). Pherekydes and Sappho are both drawing upon a vestiary code that regulates female decency in the ancient world. The head is its focus. Headgear is crucial to female honor, an index of sexual purity and civilized status. No decent woman should be seen in public wihout her headdress; only prostitutes and maenads run about unveiled. When Sappho regrets she cannot cover her daughter's head properly she is recording a personal chaos that extends from the boundaries of the body to the edge of civility—the edge where it all leaks away.

See also fr. 81b (above) where Sappho says the Graces despise a woman whose head is without a crown. We might note in passing that the most common Greek word for what veils a female head is *krēdemnon,* whose symbolic force can be read from its threefold usage. Properly signifying a woman's "headbinder," *krēdemnon* is also used to mean "battlements of a city" and "stopper of a bottle." It is plain what these three have in common. A corked bottle, a fortified city, a veiled woman are vessels sealed against dirt and loss. To put the lid on certifies purity.

98b.1 "Kleis": given as the name of Sappho's daughter in ancient sources.

Fragments 98a and 98b represent the top and bottom, respectively, of the same papyrus column. The first three lines of 98b stand at the foot of the column with a horizontal stroke appended to each in the left margin, which Voigt takes to signify that they were omitted from their proper place above.

98b.7 "the Kleanaktidai": the name of the ruling family of the city of Mytilene during Sappho's lifetime. Testimonia suggest that Sappho was exiled from Lesbos to Sicily around 600 B.C., presumably because she fell out of favor with this faction. The poem may be a lament from exile. Sappho regrets something "terribly leaked away" in the final verse, and the loss is figured in earlier verses as absence of a spangled headbinder for Kleis. This item of apparel is evidently unavailable in Sicily although, in the good old days in Mytilene, Sappho's mother used to talk about proper techniques for binding the hair and would have seen to it that Kleis got what a girl needs. Exile frustrates such needs, dislocates the style of life that depends on them. In this poem style is a deep need.

101.1 "handcloths": this obscure term (sometimes translated "napkin") is a compound of the word for "hand" and the word for "cloth" but Athenaios insists that Sappho means it as "an adornment for the head," citing the historian Hekataios who reports that women wore this item on their heads (*Deipnosophistai* 9.410e).

102.2 "slender": not an attribute of Aphrodite generally in literature or art, so some editors emend the text and transfer the adjective to the boy.

104a Cited by the literary critic Demetrios, who comments: "Here the charm of the expression lies in its repetition of 'gather'" (*On Style* 141). Catullus imitates these verses in a poem that is a wedding song (see his poem 62, especially vv. 20–37); maybe Sappho's poem is nuptial too—telling of the pathos of the bride one fine evening when the repetitions of childhood end. I read somewhere once that ancient marriage rites may have included a burning of the axle of the chariot that brought the bride to her bridegroom's house—no going back.

105a.1 "as": the poem begins in a simile which has no *comparandum* and a relative clause which never reaches completion in a main verb. It may be an epithalamium; Himerios refers to these verses in a discussion of wedding songs ("Sappho likens a girl to an apple" *Orations* 9.16) and George Eliot mentions them in connection with Mrs. Cadwallader's marriage plans for Celia and Sir James ("for he was not one of those gentlemen who languish after the unattainable Sappho's apple laughing from the topmost bough": *Middlemarch,* chapter 6). If there is a bride here she remains inaccessible; it is her inaccessibility that is present, grammatically and erotically. Desiring hands close upon empty air in the final infinitive.

105a.1–2 "high . . . high . . . highest": I have stretched out the line to imitate a trajectory of reaching that is present in the sound of the Greek *(akro . . . akron . . . akrotato)* and in the rhythm (dactyls slow to spondees) as the apple begins to look farther and farther away.

105a.2–3 "forgot—no, not forgot": self-correction emphasizes desire's infinite deferral. Self-correction is also apparent in the Greek prosody of the poem, which includes seven instances of correption or elision, metrical tactics designed to restrain a unit of sound from reaching beyond its own position in the rhythm. (Elision is the cutting away of a vowel at the end of a word when it is contiguous with a vowel at the start of the next word. Correption is the shortening of a long vowel or diphthong, from two beats to one, before a following vowel). Three of these instances affect the ardent preposition *epi* which can express location or motion: "on, upon, to, toward, aiming at, reaching after." The final infinitive is a compound of this preposition: *epikesthai.*

105b Comparison with an epithalamium of Catullus (62.39–47) has suggested to some editors that this fragment intends an image of defloration.

106 Cited by Demetrios *On Style* (146); other ancient commentators tell us that the expression "compared to the Lesbian singer" became proverbial.

107 Cited by Apollonios Dyskolos in a treatise *On Conjunctions* (490).

117b Hymenaios is god of weddings. Ancient commentaries speak of Sappho as having composed either eight or nine books of poems, of which one book consisted entirely of epithalamia. Frr. 27, 30, 44, 110–117b, 141 may be from that book. It is unclear whether Sappho's epithalamia were intended for presentation at actual weddings or as a literary indulgence of the nuptial mood. There is no evidence how these songs might have been performed, in public or in private, by Sappho herself or a choir.

121 Stobaeus cites this fragment and tells us that it refers to the relative ages of marriage partners (4.22). Here is an example of the intractability of pronouns discussed in fr. 38 above. Sappho's text has "you" in the singular and "us" in the plural. If this seems inapt, change "us" to "me."

See M. Kaimio, *The Chorus of Greek Drama within the Light of the Person and Number Used* (Helsinki, 1970), 30; A. Lardinois, "Who Sang Sappho's Songs?" in E. Greene, ed., *Reading Sappho* (Berkeley, 1996), 160–4.

124 Cited by Hephaistion in his metrical *Handbook* as an example of a measure called "prosodiac."

125 Cited by the scholiast on Aristophanes *Thesmophoriazousai* (401) who tells us "weaving garlands was done by young people and those in love."

126 Cited by the *Etymologicum Genuinum* for its use of an unusual word for "sleep." The word translated "friend" is *hetaira*, on which see note to fr. 142 below.

130.1 "(now again)": see above frr. 1 and 22.

130.2 "unmanageable": a word made from the root *machan-* (cf. English "machine") and cognate with words for "contrivance, device, instrument, means, technique." Eros is a creature against whom no technology avails.

131 Voigt prints frr. 130 and 131 together as one poem. Most editors separate them. Our source for all four lines is Hephaistion, who cites them without a break (and without any author's name) as examples of the same meter (*Handbook* 7.7).

132 Cited by Hephaistion in his metrical *Handbook* as an example of four kinds of trochaic dimeter—procatalectic, acatalectic, hypercatalectic and brachycatalectic—combined into an *asyntartete* or "unconnected" meter (15.18).

On this exceptionally obscure meter see D. L. Page, *Sappho and Alcaeus* (Oxford, 1955), 131 n. 4.

133.2 Sappho's name is in the vocative case. To apostrophize oneself this way is very unusual: I cannot find another example of it in Greek lyric poetry. Possibly the apostrophe is meant to be contained within the speech of someone else, as in fr. 1 where Aphrodite addresses Sappho by name.

134 Cited by Hephaistion in his metrical *Handbook* as an example of acatalectic ionic trimeter (12.4).

Kyprogeneia is an epithet of Aphrodite meaning "born on Kypros."

135 Cited by Hephaistion in his metrical *Handbook* as an example of the fact that "whole songs were written in ionic meter by Alkman and Sappho" (12.2).

Pandion was a king of Athens who had two daughters, Prokne and Philomela, one of whom was the wife of Tereus, while the other was raped by Tereus, who cut out her tongue so she could not tell. Silenced, she wove a cloth to reveal her sad story, which her sister read and, to punish Tereus, killed their only child (Itys). Both girls were turned into birds, one into a swallow and one into a nightingale, according to Ovid whose version does not make clear which is which (*Metamorphoses* 6.412–674). There are other ancient versions of this myth, including one where the killing of Itys is inadvertent: cf. Homer *Odyssey* 19.518–29 and Sappho fr. 136 below and note.

136 A Sophoklean scholiast cites this verse, reminding us that Sophokles has the expression "messenger of Zeus" of the nightingale because it signals the coming of spring (*Elektra* 149). Sophokles also calls the nightingale "bewildered by grief" and Homer has Penelope compare herself to this sorrowful bird of spring (*Odyssey* 19.518–29). Aristotle describes the nightingale as having no tip on its tongue (*Historia animalium* 616b8): cf. note on fr. 135 above.

137 Aristotle cites these verses in a discussion of shame (*Rhetoric* 1367a). He appears to think they represent an interchange between Sappho and the poet Alkaios. Some editors take this to mean that Alkaios is being quoted in the first two verses; others read the poem as Sappho's response to some poem of Alkaios that she didn't like. The meter of the verses is Alkaic, of which there is no other example in Sappho.

The word translated "shame" in the first and fifth lines of the fragment is much more interesting in Greek: *aidōs* (also rendered "reverence, respect, shame-fastness, awe, sense of honor") is a sort of voltage of decorum that radiates from the boundaries of people and makes them instantly sensitive to one another's status and mood. Proverbially it is a phenomenon of vision and the opposite of *hybris*:

> *Aidōs* lives upon the eyelids of sensitive people, *hybris* upon those of the insensitive. An intelligent person knows this.
>
> —Stobaios 4.230

Aidōs can also connote the mutual shyness felt by lover and beloved in an erotic encounter, which soon becomes an enclosure shutting out the world:

> Aphrodite . . .
> cast upon their sweet bed the shamefastness of eros,
> fitting together and mingling in marriage
> the god and the girl.
>
> —Pindar *Pythians* 9.9–13

138 Athenaios tells us that Sappho addressed these words "to a man who is extravagantly admired for his physique and regarded as beautiful" (*Deipnosophistai* 13.564d).

140.1 "delicate": this word also means "soft, luxurious, expensive, dainty, refined" and carries connotations of aristocracy, sensuality and the East. On the social and political implications of the adjective and its cognate noun *abrosynē*, see above fr. 58 and note.

140.2 Kythereia is a name of Aphrodite.

For Adonis see also fr. 168 and Appendix (below) on Phaon. The myth of Adonis tells how Aphrodite fell in love with a beautiful mortal youth. One day while they are out hunting together Adonis is gored in the thigh by a wild bull and dies. Aphrodite mourns him. In some versions Aphrodite lays the dying Adonis in a bed of lettuces (anthropologically provocative since lettuces were said to cause impotence: see Marcel Detienne, *The Gardens of Adonis,* translated by J. Lloyd [New York, 1972]). The Hellenistic poet Dioskourides calls Sappho a "fellow mourner" with Aphrodite in her grief over Adonis (*Palatine Anthology* 7.407)—presumably referring to fr. 140, which seems to be a dialogue between worshippers and Aphrodite, and is the earliest evidence we have of an Adonis cult. This cult traveled from Syria to Asia Minor to Athens, where it was celebrated in the fifth and fourth centuries B.C. in a festival called the Adonia. Historians have reconstructed the Athenian Adonia largely from vase paintings: women planted seeds of lettuce, fennel, wheat or barley in pots. Once the seeds had sprouted the pots were carried up to the roofs of houses where the sprouts shriveled in the sun and the women lamented. Then the pots were thrown into the sea. Dancing to flutes and tambourines took place. The Adonia was also celebrated at Alexandria in the third and second centuries B.C., according to Theokritos, who describes Queen Arsinoe's version: images of Aphrodite and Adonis reclining together on a banquet couch surrounded by fruit were venerated while a singer told Adonis' story. Then the image of Adonis was thrown into the sea with much lamenting (Theokritos *Idyll* 15). There is historical evidence of fervent celebration of this rite as late as the fourth century A.D.: when Julian made a tour of the Near East shortly after his elevation to emperor in 362 A.D., his entry into Antioch was seriously offset by wild ululations of grief from streets and houses. He had coincided with the Adonia, whose observance persisted in the largely Christian city as one of its many festivals (Ammianus Marcellinus 22.9.15).

See Wahib Atallah, *Adonis dans la littérature et l'art grec* (Paris, 1966); G. W. Bowersock, *Julian the Apostate* (Cambridge, Mass., 1978).

141 Athenaios cites these lines to support his claim that both Sappho and Alkaios call Hermes the wine pourer of the gods (*Deipnosophistai* 10.425d; cf. Alkaios fr. 447).

142 "friends" *(hetairai):* cited by Athenaios (*Deipnosophistai* 13.471d) in a discussion of the word *hetaira*, which began to be used in the sixth century B.C. as the term for "courtesan" or "mistress" (distinct from *pornē*, "whore") within the elite sexual commodity trade of the male symposium. In Sappho's language, however *hetaira* appears to connote a close female companion or intimate friend in a relationship that may be sexual but is not commoditized (cf. frr. 126 and 160).

On these terms and values see J. N. Davidson, *Courtesans and Fishcakes: Th Consuming Passions of Classical Athens* (London, 1997); K. J. Dover, *Greek Homo sexuality* (Cambridge, Mass., 1989); L. Kurke, *Coins, Bodies, Games and Gol* (Princeton, 1999); C. Reinsberg, *Ehe, Hetärentum und Knabenliebe im antike*

Griechenland (Munich, 1989); A. Richlin, ed., *Pornography and Representation in Greece and Rome* (Oxford, 1992).

143 Cited by Athenaios in a discussion of chickpeas (*Deipnosophistai* 2.54f).

144.2 This phrase is preserved for us by the grammarian Herodian in his treatise *On the Declension of Nouns* because he is interested in the way Gorgo's name is declined. For other information about Gorgo see above fr. 29c and notes to frr. 8, 22 and 155.

145 By "stones" Sappho means a heap of small stones or gravel, according to the scholiast who cites this phrase, and she may be quoting a proverb. Gravel seems to have had a lively proverbial life, e.g., Alkaios fr. 344LP:

> I know for sure if a man moves gravel—tricky stone to work with—he gets a sore head.

146 In a rhetorical treatise *On Figures of Speech* (25) the first-century-B.C. grammarian Tryphon preserves this phrase as an example of a proverb; its proverbial sense is interpreted by the second-century-A.D. lexicographer Diogenian: "used of those unwilling to take the good with the bad" (*Proverbs* 6.58). Since bees and honey are frequently associated with Aphrodite in ancient cult and religious symbology, the proverb may also imply a renunciation of things aphrodisiac.

Other translations occur to me, e.g.:

> mellowsmelling honey
> yellowstinging bee
> honey, Honey?
> no not me

147.1 It may be of interest that this verse contains an emendation by the sixteenth-century classical scholar Isaac Casaubon, perhaps the model for George Eliot's character of the same surname, whom she calls "a Bat of erudition" (*Middlemarch*, chapter 21). The real Casaubon was one of the two great Huguenots who dominated classical scholarship in Europe at the close of the sixteenth century; the other one was Joseph Scaliger to whom is ascribed the remark, regarding

Casaubon's edition of Persius, "The sauce is better than the fish." Casaubon was born in Geneva of refugee parents and had to learn his Greek while hiding in a cave in the French mountains (with bats?). He died in exile in England. Casaubon's emendation of *mnasasthai* to *mnasesthai* in fr. 147 ("did remember" to "will remember") is generally accepted, if dull, and makes me think of George Eliot's final assertion in the novel:

Every limit is a beginning as well as an ending.
— "Finale," *Middlemarch* (London, 1871); see also M. Pattison,
Isaac Casaubon 1559–1614 (Oxford, 1892)

148 Cited by a scholiast to explain Pindar's gnomic saying:

Wealth ornamented with virtues brings the right occasion for all sorts of things.
— *Olympians* 2.96–7

150 Maximus of Tyre provides some domestic insight on this fragment, amid his comparison of Sappho and Sokrates:

Sokrates blazed up at Xanthippe for lamenting when he was dying, as did Sappho at her daughter.
— *Orations* 18.9

155 Cited by Maximus of Tyre in his comparison of Sappho and Sokrates to show how

sometimes she rebukes them [Gorgo and Andromeda], sometimes she interrogates them and sometimes she uses irony just like Sokrates when he says: *Farewell to you, Ion!*
— *Orations* 18.9, referring to the opening words of Plato's *Ion*

156 Demetrios (*On Style* 161) quotes these phrases in a discussion of hyperbole pointing out that "every hyperbole involves the impossible" and comparing phrase from Aristophanes like "healthier than a pumpkin" and "balder than a clear sky."

He congratulates Sappho on her talent for using the impossible gracefully, not frigidly. No such approval is given by Gregory of Corinth (On Hermogenes):

Erotic phrases like these from Anakreon and Sappho flatter the ear shamefully: whiter than milk, smoother than water, more songlike than lyres, prouder than a mare, more delicate than roses, softer than a robe, more expensive than gold!

158 Plutarch cites this advice of Sappho's in his essay On Restraining Anger:

When people are drinking the one who is silent is a pain and a burden to his comrades but amidst anger nothing is more dignified than quiet, so Sappho tells us.

—Moralia 456e

163 This phrase, followed by the words "as Sappho says," is found in a letter attributed to the emperor Julian (but probably not genuine) and addressed to a certain Eugenios the philosopher (Epistles 386c). Julian (or his interpolator) seems to have liked Sappho; see also frr. 34 and 48 above.

165 Cited by the grammarian Apollonios Dyskolos in a treatise On Pronouns (106a) and believed by some to be a more correct reading of fr. 31.1 (in place of "that man seems to me").

166 Cited by Athenaios (Deipnosophistai 2.57d) in order to comment on the spelling of the word for "egg." This egg may be the one from which Kastor, Pollux, Helen and Klytemnestra were born, although swan's eggs are whitish not blue.

168 Cited by Marius Plotius Sacerdos in his Art of Grammar (3.3) as an example of the metrical shape called an adonius (or catalectic dactylic dimeter, i.e., a dactyl followed by a sponde: – ⌣ ⌣ – –), which was invented by Sappho and typically forms the fourth verse of a Sapphic stanza.

168A According to Zenobios in his Proverbs (3.3) Gello was the name of a girl who died untimely young "and her ghost haunts little children (so the Lesbians say) and they ascribe young deaths to her."

168B Cited by Hephaistion in his metrical *Handbook* (11.5) as two tetrameter verses without authorial ascription; cited by Apostolius and his son Arsenius, compilers of proverbs in the fifteenth century, as Sappho's; not included among Sappho's fragments by most modern editors.

168C Cited without authorial ascription by Demetrios *On Style* (164) as an example of gracefulness of language produced by use of beautiful names; not regarded as Sapphic by most modern editors except Wilamowitz *Sappho und Simonides* (Berlin, 1913), 46.

169 From here to the end Voigt's edition prints glosses, i.e., single words cited as Sappho's without context by various ancient authorities.

172 **"paingiver" or perhaps "whose gift is pain"**: a Sapphic epithet of Eros, according to Maximus of Tyre (*Orations* 18.9). He cites this word along with *glukupikron* ("sweetbitter": see above fr. 130 cf. frr. 8 and 188) in a comparison between Sappho and Plato's Diotima, whose view is that Eros "flourishes in abundance but dies away when he is in want" (*Symposium* 203b).

173 The grammarian George Choiroboskos (*On Theodosios* 1.331) cites this otherwise unknown word: *amamaxys*.

174 The lexicographer Orion cites this otherwise unknown word: *amara*.

175 Cited by Apollonios Dyskolos in a treatise *On Adverbs* (596) as an example of a metaplasm, i.e., an inflected form derived from a nonexistent nominative singular.

176 Cited by Athenaios (*Deipnosophistai* 4.182f) free-associating on different spellings of the word for "lyre."

180 "holder": or capitalized, Holder, i.e., Hektor.

188 "mythweaver": a word ascribed to Sappho by Maximus of Tyre who says:

Sokrates calls Eros "sophist," Sappho calls him "mythweaver."

—*Orations* 18.9

Mythweaver might also be rendered "teller of tales" or "creator of fictions" or "poetic inventor." Why does Eros weave myths? Perhaps because desire acts in lovers as a lure for the whole life of the imagination—without which neither love nor philosophy could nourish itself very long. According to Maximus of Tyre, one may say of Sappho no less than of Sokrates that a knowledge of erotic things is the chief pursuit of life. Sokrates claims something like this more than once in Plato's dialogues (e.g., *Symposium* 177d; *Theages* 128b); Sappho's argument is implicit. See also frr. 8 and 172 above.

WHO'S WHO

Abanthis: woman about whom nothing is known

Acheron: river of Hades

Adonis: young man loved by Aphrodite whose cult was popular with women and had something to do with lettuce

Aelian: (Claudius Aelianus) writer of miscellanies 170–235 A.D.
      Hercher, ed., *Varia Historia*

Aelius Aristides: rhetorician of the second century A.D.
      Keil, ed., *Orationes*

Aiga: promontory of Asia Minor

Alkaios: lyric poet who lived on the island of Lesbos in the seventh century B.C.
      Voigt, ed., *Sappho et Alcaeus Fragmenta*

Anakreon: lyric poet of Teos 575–490 B.C.
      Page, ed., *Poetae Melici Graeci*

Anaktoria: possibly a companion of Sappho, see fr. 16 and fr. 8 note

Andromache: wife of Hektor at Troy

Andromeda: possibly a companion of Sappho, see fr. 68a and fr. 8 note

Antiphanes: comic poet of the fourth century B.C.
      Kock, ed., *Comicorum Atticorum Fragmenta,* vol. 2

Aphrodite: goddess of love, sex and desire

Apollonios Dyskolos: grammarian of the second century A.D. who is said to have been given the name Dyskolos ("hard to digest") because of the toughness of his subject matter

> Schneider-Uhlig, eds., *Grammatici Graeci*, vol. 2

Archeanassa: member of the Archeanactid family of Lesbos

Archilochos: iambic and elegiac poet who lived on the islands of Paros and Thasos in the seventh century B.C.

> West, ed., *Iambi et Elegi Graeci*

Aristophanes: comic poet of the fifth century B.C.

Aristotle: philosopher 384–322 B.C.

Artemis: goddess of animals, hunting, wild places and female freedom

Athenaios: writer of a miscellany of literary and other anecdotes called *Deipnosophistai*

> Kaibel, ed.

Atthis: possibly a companion of Sappho, see fr. 8 and note

Atreus: father of Agamemnon and Menelaos

Catullus: lyric poet in Rome 84–54 B.C.

Chrysippos: Stoic philosopher 280–207 B.C.

> von Arnim, ed., *Stoicorum veterum fragmenta*

Comes Natalis: mythographer of the sixteenth century A.D.

> Francofen, ed., *Mythologia*

Demetrios: literary critic who lived in the first century B.C. or A.D.

> Rhys Roberts, ed., *De Elocutione*

Diehl: E. Diehl, *Anthologia Lyrica Graeca,* 3 vols. (Leipzig, 1923 and 1936)

Diels: H. Diels, *Die Fragmente der Vorsokratiker, griechisch und deutsch,* 3 vols. (Berlin, 1959–1960)

Dika: possibly a companion of Sappho, see fr. 81

Diogenian: lexicographer and paroemiographer of the second century A.D.
Leutsch-Schneidewin, eds., *Paroemiographi Graeci,* vol. 1

Dionysios of Halikarnassos: historian and grammarian of the first century B.C.
Usener-Radermacher, eds., *Opuscula*

Doricha: possibly a girlfriend of Sappho's brother, see frr. 7, 15 and notes

Eirana: possibly a companion of Sappho, see frr. 91 and 135

Eros: god of everything erotic

Etymologicum Genuinum: etymological dictionary compiled about 870 A.D. under Photios

Euboulos: comic poet of the early fourth century B.C.
Kock, ed., *Comicorum Atticorum Fragmenta,* vol. 2

Euripides: Athenian tragic poet 485–406 B.C.

Eustathios: Christian grammarian of the twelfth century A.D. who wrote commentaries on Homer

Galen: writer on medicine, philosophy and grammar who (possibly) lived in the second century A.D.
Marquardt, ed., *Galeni Scripta Minora*
Hilgard, ed., *Grammatici Graeci,* vol. 4

Gello: name of a girl who died untimely young; her ghost haunts little children

Georgios Choiroboskos: ninth-century-A.D. grammarian, deacon and ecclesiastical archivist of Constantinople

> Hilgard, ed., *Scholia in Theodosii Canones*

Geraistion: temple of Poseidon at Geraistos in Euboia

Gongyla: possibly a companion of Sappho, see fr. 22 with note and fr. 95

Gorgo: possibly a companion of Sappho, see frr. 8, 22, 29c, 144, 155 and notes

Gow-Page: A. S. F. Gow and D. L. Page, eds., *The Greek Anthology,* 2 vols. (Cambridge, 1965)

Graces: goddesses who confer grace, beauty, charm, brightness

Gregory of Corinth: grammarian of the twelfth century A.D.

> Walz, ed., *Rhetorici Graeci,* vol. 7

Gyrinno or Gyrinna: possibly a companion of Sappho, see fr. 82a and fr. 8 note

Hades: realm of the dead

Hekebolios: a sophist who taught rhetoric to Julian at Constantinople and changed his religion three times to keep up with imperial whim

Hektor: prince of Troy and husband of Andromache

Helen: wife of Menelaos and lover of Paris of Troy

Hera: wife of Zeus

Herodian: grammarian of the late second century A.D. and son of Apollonios Dyskolos

> Lentz, ed., *Grammatici Graeci,* vol. 3

Herodotos: historian of the fifth century B.C.

Hermione: daughter of Helen and Menelaos

Himerios: rhetorician of the fourth century A.D.
> Colonna, ed., *Orationes*

Hymenaios: god of weddings

Idaios: herald of Troy

Ilios: Greek name for Troy

Ilos: father of Priam, king of Troy

Julian: nephew of Constantine the Great and Roman emperor 361–363 A.D., notorious for his attempt to restore the pagan gods to primacy and for his long letters
> Bidez-Cumont, eds., *Epistolae*

Kallimachos: poet, scholar, royal librarian of the great library at Alexandria under Ptolemy Philadelphos, lived 305–240 B.C. and is said by the *Suda* to have written eight hundred volumes of prose and verse

Kalliope: first of the nine Muses, whose name means "beautiful-voiced"

Kleanakdtidai: one of the ruling clans of the city of Mytilene in Sappho's lifetime

Kleis: alleged name of Sappho's mother and also of her daughter

Koos: father of Leto

Krete: Crete

Kronos: father of Zeus

Kypris: name of Aphrodite as one worshipped on the island of Kypros (Cyprus)

Kyprogeneia: epithet of Aphrodite ("Kypros-born")

Kypros: Cyprus

Kythereia: name of Aphrodite as one associated with the city of Kythera in Krete

Leto: mother of Apollo and Artemis

Libanius: rhetorician, 314–393 A.D.
      Förster, ed., *Orationes*

Longinus: literary critic of the first century A.D. whose authorship of *On the Sublime* is now disputed
      Roberts, ed., *De Sublimitate*

LP: Lobel, E., and D. L. Page, eds., *Poetarum Lesbiorum Fragmenta* (Oxford, 1955)

Lydia: kingdom of western Asia Minor legendary for luxury

Marius Plotius Sacerdos: metrician and grammarian of the third century A.D.
      Keil, ed., *Grammatici Latini,* vol. 6

Marsyas (the younger): historian of (probably) the first century A.D.

Maximus of Tyre: rhetorician and itinerant lecturer of the second century A.D.
      Hobein, ed., *Orationes*

Medeia: princess of Kolchis and wife of Jason

Megara: possibly a companion of Sappho, see fr. 68a and fr. 8 note

Menander: comic poet 342–293 B.C.
      Kock, ed., *Comicorum Atticorum Fragmenta,* vol. 3

Mika: possibly a companion of Sappho, see fr. 71

Mnasadika: see fr. 82

Muses: goddesses of music, song, dance, poetry and erudition who were numbered at nine but Sappho is sometimes called the tenth (e.g., *Palatine Anthology* 7.14 and 9.506)

Mytilene: chief city of the island of Lesbos and home of Sappho

Nereids: nymphs of the sea, all fifty of them supposedly daughters of Nereus

Niobe: Theban woman killed by Artemis and Apollo after she boasted to Leto of the number of her children

Olympos: mountain where dwell the Olympian gods

Orion: lexicographer of the fifth century A.D.
      Sturz, ed.

Palaiphatos: mythographer of the fourth century B.C.
      Festa, ed., *Mythographi Graeci*, vol. 3

Palatine Anthology: collection of epigrams by various Greek poets compiled about 980 A.D. from earlier collections
      Gow-Page, ed., *The Greek Anthology*

Pan: god of flocks and herds and outdoor amusements usually depicted as a man with goat's feet, horns and shaggy hair

Pandion: king of Athens and father of Prokne and Philomela; the former was the wife of Tereus; the latter was raped by Tereus, who cut out her tongue so she could not tell

Panormos: city of (possibly) Sicily

Paon: epithet of Apollo

Paphos: city of Kypros near which Aphrodite originally emerged from the sea

Parian Marble: marble column inscribed with important events of Greek history to 263 B.C. and from which certain information about the lives of ancient poets has been derived

Penthelids: one of the clans struggling for power in Mytilene in the seventh century B.C. and who claimed descent from Penthilos, son of Orestes

Pherekydes: pre-Sokratic philosopher of the sixth century B.C.
    Diels, ed., *Die Fragmente der Vorsokratiker, griechisch und deutsch,* vol. 2

Phoibos: adjective meaning "pure bright radiant beaming," used as epithet of Apollo

Phokaia: city of western Asia Minor

Photios: lexicographer and patriarch of Constantinople in the ninth century A.D.
    Reitzenstein, ed., *Lexicon*

Pieria: region of northern Greece where the Muses live

Plakia: river near the city of Thebe

Pleiades: group of seven stars

Pliny (the elder): Roman encyclopaedist 23–79 A.D.

Pollux: lexicographer and rhetorician of the second century A.D.
    Bethe, ed.

Polyanaktides: son of Polyanax and member of the Polyanaktid family of Lesbos

Posidippos: Greek poet of the third century B.C.
    Gow-Page, ed., *The Greek Anthology*

Priam: king of Troy

Sapphic stanza: stanzaic form invented by Sappho that is composed of three hendecasyllabic (eleven-syllable) verses followed by one adonean (five-syllable) verse

Seneca: Roman philosopher and poet 4 B.C.–65 A.D.

Stobaios: anthologist of the early fifth century A.D.
    Wachsmuth-Hense, eds.

Strabo: geographer of the first century A.D.
    Kramer, ed.

Suda: lexicon compiled in Byzantium in the tenth century A.D.
    Adler, ed.

Terentianus Maurus: grammarian and metrician of the late second century A.D.
    Keil, ed., *Grammatici Latini,* vol. 6

Thebe: city of Asia Minor where Andromache lived before she married Hektor

Thyone: mortal woman also known as Semele who bore Dionysos to Zeus

Tryphon: grammarian of the first century B.C.
    Spengel, ed., *Rhetores Graeci,* vol. 3

Tyndarids: descendants of Tyndareus, king of Sparta, who fathered Helen, Klytemnestra, Kastor, Pollux

Zeus: king of gods and father of (among others) Aphrodite

APPENDIX: SOME EXEMPLARY TESTIMONIA

·

The fourth-century-B.C. comic poet Antiphanes produced a comedy called *Sappho*
in which Sappho appears as a character and poses this riddle with its answer:

> There is a female creature who hides in her womb unborn children,
> and although the infants are voiceless they cry out across the waves
>   of the sea
> and over the whole earth to whomever they wish
> and people who are not present and even deaf people can hear them.
> The female creature is a letter
> and the infants she carries are the letters of the alphabet:
> although voiceless they can speak to those far away,
> to whomever they wish whereas if someone happens to be
> standing right next to the reader he will not hear.
>
> —*Comicorum Atticorum Fragmenta* fr. 196 Kock

On the riddle see Y. Prins, *Victorian Sappho* (Princeton, 1999), 23–7; J. Svenbro,
Phrasikleia, translated by J. Lloyd (Ithaca, 1993), 158–86.

·

Three poems of the *Palatine Anthology* are ascribed to Sappho (probably wrongly):

> Children, although I am voiceless I answer anyone who asks
>   since I have a tireless voice set at my feet:
> to Aithopia daughter of Leto I was dedicated by Arista
>   daughter of Hermokleides son of Saunaiadas.
> She is your handmaid, queen of women. Rejoice in her
>   and be gracious to our famous family.
>
>   6.269

Of Timas here is the dust, dead before marriage,
                received in Persephone's darkblue chamber
        and when she died all her friends with newsharpened knife
                took the lovely hair from their heads.

                                                                7.489

            On the tomb of Pelagon his father Meniskos put
                    basket and oar, memories of sad life.

                                                                7.505

                                    .

Data on the mysterious Phaon:

Phaon had no life except his boat and his sea. His sea was a strait. No one
complained, since he was in fact a moderate man and accepted money only
from the rich. There was amazement among the Lesbians about his way of
life. The goddess (they mean Aphrodite) wanted to thank this man so she put
on the appearance of an old woman and asked Phaon about crossing the
strait. He at once carried her across and asked nothing in return. What did
the goddess do then? She transformed him (they say) from an old man—
repaid him with youth and beauty. This is the Phaon whom Sappho loved and
celebrated in lyric song.

                            —Palaiphatos *On Incredible Things* 211a

The temple of Apollo at Leukas [is the site of] the leap believed to put an
end to desire: "where Sappho first of all" (so Menander says) "pursuing
proud Phaon was so stung by love that she threw herself from the far-seen
cliff. . . ." So it was the custom among the Leukadians at the annual festival
of Apollo that some criminal be thrown from the cliff, with all kinds of wings
and birds fastened to him to break his fall and many people in small boats
waiting below in a circle to save him and take him off beyond the borders.

                —Strabo *Geography* 10.2.9; see also Menander fr. 258 Koerte

Phaon the most beautiful of men was hid by Aphrodite amid lettuces.

                                —Aelian *Historical Miscellanies* 12.18

Kallimachos says Aphrodite hid Adonis in a bed of lettuces. . . . Euboulos in *The Impotent Men* says: ". . . for it was amid vegetables, so the story goes, that the Kyprian laid out dead Adonis." Kratinos says that when Aphrodite fell in love with Phaon she hid him among "beautiful lettuces." Marsyas says it was green barley.

—Athenaios *Deipnosophistai* 2.69e–d

Sappho has left a written record that dead Adonis was laid out among lettuces by Aphrodite.

—Comes Natalis *Mythology* 5.16

Strange lore about the plant called *ēryngē* ("sea holly"): its root takes the shape of the male or the female sex organ. It is rarely found but if men happen upon the male shape they become desirable; on this account Phaon of Lesbos was desired by Sappho.

—Pliny *Natural History* 22.20

Many people say Sappho fell in love with Phaon—not Sappho the poet but [some other] Lesbian woman—and when she didn't get him she threw herself off the cliff of Leukas.

—Photios *Lexicon*

.

A second-century-A.D. papyrus furnishes a putative list of first words of poems by Alkaios, Anakreon or Sappho:

> here to me island
> two loves me
> we stand prayer
> O you who welcomed
> holy much-
> queen of heaven
> Eros was entertained
> here blessed ones
> who of desire
> already profit

hail you of Kyllene
the big sea
let us sacrifice to Aphrodite
to Danaos
holy mother
Kyprian
let Aphrodite set free
let her awake
varied voice
keep away the wind
sweet
hail hail
I saw
I entreat
new
O child
come
O

.

The *Palatine Anthology* includes two epitaphs for Sappho:

On Sappho you lie, Aeolian earth, who amid the immortal
    Muses sings as a mortal Muse,
whom Kypris and Eros reared together, with whom Persuasion
    wove an everliving Pierian crown,
for Greece a delight, for you a glory. O Fates who twist
    triple thread on your spindle,
how is it you did not spin out an utterly deathless day
    for the one who devised deathless gifts of the Muses?
—Antipater of Sidon *Palatine Anthology* 7.14

As you bypass the Aeolian tomb, stranger, do not say I am dead,
    I the songmaker of Mytilene.
For hands of men made this and such human works
    vanish into quick oblivion.

But if you rate me by the grace of the Muses, from each of whom
      I put a flower beside my own nine,
you will realize I escaped the shadowland of Hades nor will there be
      a sunlit day that lacks the name of lyric Sappho.

              —Tullius Laurea *Palatine Anthology* 7.17

.

Last word from Seneca:

Didymus the grammarian wrote four thousand books: I would feel sorry for
him if he had merely *read* so much verbiage. His books investigate questions
like the birthplace of Homer, the real mother of Aeneas, if Anakreon was more
of a lecher than a drunk, whether Sappho was a whore, etc. etc. etc. And
people complain that life is short!

              —*Epistles* 88.37